Beginning Apple Watch Development

1st Edition

Introduction

Welcome! Congratulations to taking the first step to creating amazing Apple Watch applications!

The Apple Watch leverages on the iOS platform and this easy-to-follow book walks you through the development process of Watch apps step by step. This book explores simple basics to moderate aspects of Apple Watch application development.

In it, we teach you how to download the tools, get Xcode up and running, code Apple Watch applications, submit your app to the App Store and share your finished app with the world.

Who this book is written for

This book is written for the beginning Apple Watch developer. It would be great if you have some basic background in programming. But if you don't, do not worry as I explain fundamental programming concepts from the ground up.

How this book is structured

In this book, we break down Apple Watch programming into smaller chunks which make individual chapters. Each chapter and its code examples are generally independent from those in earlier chapters (except for chapters 7 and 8) so this gives you the flexibility to go directly to topics that you are interested in.

What tools do I need?

You will need a Mac capable of running Xcode. Though having a real Apple Watch device would be useful, it is not necessary.

Source Code

Just drop us an email at support@i-ducate.com and we will send all source code to you!

Contact

We look forward to hearing from you at support@i-ducate.com. Now wait no further and get started on your Apple Watch development learning journey!

Chapter 1: Getting Started

Install Xcode

In order to develop Apple Watch apps, you need to install Xcode. Xcode is Apple's development software, which is necessary in order to build apps on iOS and OSX platforms.

Xcode is freely available on the Mac App Store. Xcode only runs on a Mac, you will not be able to develop Apple Watch apps (and iOS apps in general) on other platforms, like Windows or Linux PC.

What You Will Need

A Mac running OS X Yosemite (10.10) or higher

We will use Xcode 6.3 for developing Apple Watch apps. Xcode 6.3 requires OS X Yosemite or higher. Yosemite is a free upgrade and runs on most Macs.

An Apple ID

You also need a free App Store account, which is also referred to as an Apple ID. You can use the same Apple ID you use to purchase apps on the App Store or sign into iCloud. If you don't have an Apple ID yet, sign up for a free ID at https:// appleid.apple.com/.

Xcode is freely available on the Mac App Store. It's a large download (over 2.6 GB), so it might take some time to download even if you have good Internet connection.

To start the download process, go to the following URL using your web browser https://itunes.apple.com/us/app/xcode/id497799835?mt=12

The Mac App Store should open up automatically, if it doesn't, you need to click the button "View in Mac App Store" (Figure 1-1).

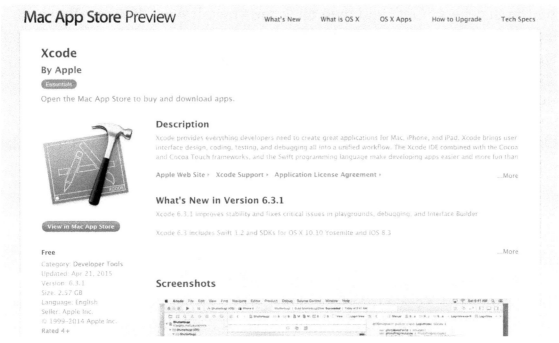

Figure 1-1

You will be redirected to the Mac App Store (Figure 1-2).

Figure 1-2

Click the button that says "Get" and then click the "Install App" button. You will be prompted to sign in to your App Store account. Use the Apple ID you created earlier to sign in.

Once you login with your Apple ID, the download will start. You can check the download progress from the Purchases tab. Once the download is finished, you will see "Open" next to the Xcode in Purchases tab. Click "Open" to launch Xcode and follow the on screen instructions to finish the installation process.

The Xcode Interface

In this section, we will have a quick look at the Xcode Interface. Getting familiar with the Xcode Interface is essential. We will create a new Xcode project to explore different areas of Xcode Interface. This Xcode project will be the simplest iOS app, which just displays an empty white screen. It might not be obvious to you the reason behind creating the iOS app, after all you are here to learn Apple Watch app development. But in order to create an Apple Watch app, you must have an existing iOS app. You can't create a standalone Apple Watch app.

The first step is to open up Xcode. If you don't see Xcode in your Dock, click the Spotlight search icon in the upper-right corner of your screen and type in Xcode. Press the return key to open Xcode and you will see the Xcode icon on your Dock. It might be a good idea to keep Xcode in your Dock, as you will need to open Xcode frequently.

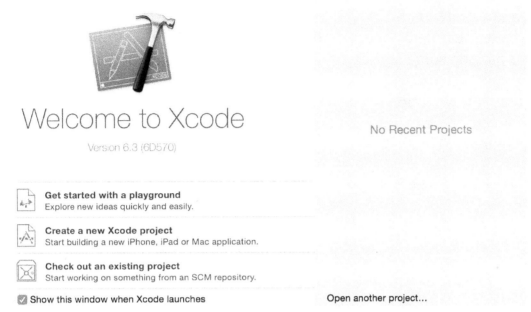

Figure 1-3

From the Xcode welcome screen (Figure 1-3), click "Create a New Xcode Project". The next screen will prompt you to choose a template for your new project.

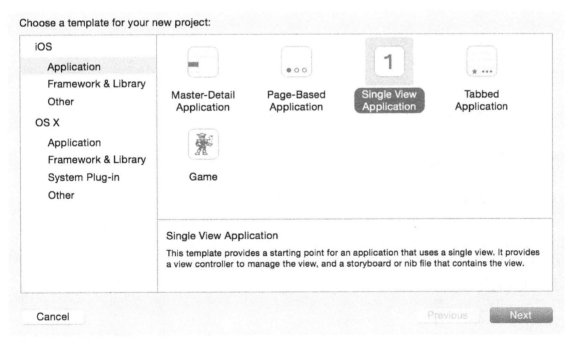

Figure 1-4

11

As you can see, there are a few different template types offered by Xcode. Based on your selected template, Xcode will create a pre-configured project. This new project will include some source code files, which are handy as a starting point.

From the template selection screen (Figure 1-4), select "Single View Application" and press "Next". This will open a new screen for you to enter options for your new app (Figure 1-5).

Choose options for your new project:

Product Name:	XcodeInterfaceDemo
Organization Name:	Pawprints Learning Technologies
Organization Identifier:	com.example
Bundle Identifier:	com.example.XcodeInterfaceDemo
Language:	Swift
Devices:	iPhone
	Use Core Data

Cancel   Previous   Next

Figure 1-5

Let me go through each of these options -

Product Name: This is the name of your app, enter *XcodeInterfaceDemo*.
Organization Name: Enter your own name or name of your company.
Organization Identifier: Organization identifier is the domain name written in reverse order. So if you own the domain *example.com*, you will use *com.example* as organization identifier. If you don't have a domain, you can pick something that seems unique to you or simply use your name. You can change this later.
Bundle Identifier: This field is auto populated by combining the *Product Name* field and *Organization Identifier* field.
Language: *Swift*
Devices: *iPhone*
Use Core Data: Leave this *unchecked*

Press **Next**. Xcode will ask you where to save your project. Though you can select any convenient location you like, it makes things easier if you create a dedicated folder for all of your apps. After you select the desired location to save project, press the **Create** button to finish the application creation process.

Xcode will automatically create a new folder for your project with the **Product Name** (*XcodeInterfaceDemo* in your case). The newly created project named *XcodeInterfaceDemo* will be opened in your Xcode project window (Figure 1-6).

Figure 1-6

As you can see, there's a lot of information crammed into this project window. It's important to get familiar with this project window, as you will be spending most of your iOS development time here.

At the top of the Xcode project window, there is a **toolbar**, which has different controls to run/stop project, select different editor, show/hide different panes etc. Below the toolbar, you can see three panes. The left one is the **Navigator** pane, the middle one is the **Editor** pane and the right one is the **Utility** pane.

The Toolbar

The top of the Xcode project window is called the **toolbar** (Figure 1-7). On the left side of the toolbar, there are controls to start and stop running your project. There is also a pop-up menu to select the **scheme** (a scheme is simply a collection of target and build settings for your project).

Figure 1-7

The middle section of the toolbar (the big box) is known as the **Activity View**. It displays any actions that are currently happening to this project, including indication of errors or warning.

On the right side of the toolbar, there are two sets of buttons. The left set lets you switch between different editors. The first of that group is the **Standard Editor**, which you will use most of the time. The standard editor gives you a single pane dedicated to editing a file. The second one is the **Assistant Editor**, which splits the editor area into two panes. The assistant editor is incredibly powerful and lets you work on two files at the same window. The third one is the **Version Editor**, which is helpful when you work with version control systems like Git.

To the right of the editor buttons, you will see another set of three buttons. Those are toggle buttons that let you show or hide left/right/bottom pane of editor pane. You will find those useful if you don't have a large monitor.

The Navigator Pane

Just below the toolbar, on the left side of the project window, is the **Navigator** pane (Figure 1-8).

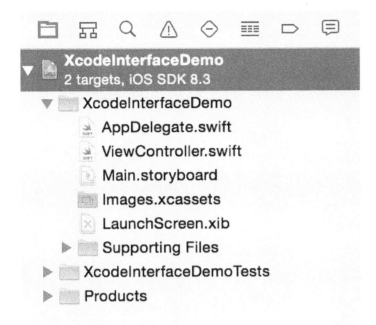

Figure 1-8

At the top of navigator pane, there are eight buttons, which corresponds to eight different navigator views. Each of these navigator view allows you to navigate different aspects of your project. Among these eight navigators, the first one is the **Project Navigator**. This navigator shows a list of files in your project. This navigator allows you to access all the code files, artworks, storyboard, data models and other project files. If you click any file in the project navigator, that file will be displayed in the editor area and you will be able to edit it.

You can switch between other navigators by simply clicking the corresponding navigator button at the top of navigator pane. Other navigators include symbol navigator, find navigator, issue navigator, test navigator and so on. Feel free to explore them and familiarize yourself. We will discuss about other navigators as we progress through other chapters of the book.

The Editor Pane

The middle pane of Xcode project window is the **Editor** pane. The editor pane displays the file you select from the **Navigator** pane. Depending upon the type of file selected, Xcode will show proper type of Editor. For example, if you select the Storyboard file, Xcode will show the visual Interface editor (Figure 1-9). Similarly, if you select a Swift file, it will show the code editor.

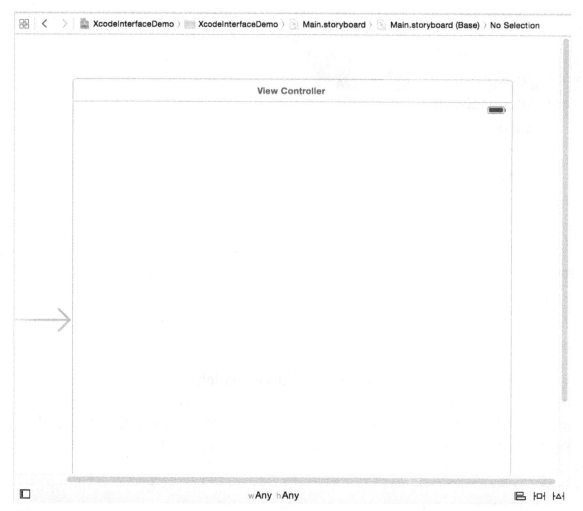

Figure 1-9

The Utility Pane

In the right pane of Xcode project window is the **Utility** pane (Figure 1-10). The upper part of the utility pane is a context-sensitive inspector, with contents that change depending upon what is being displayed in the editor area. The lower part of the utility pane contains different types of resources that you can drag into your project.

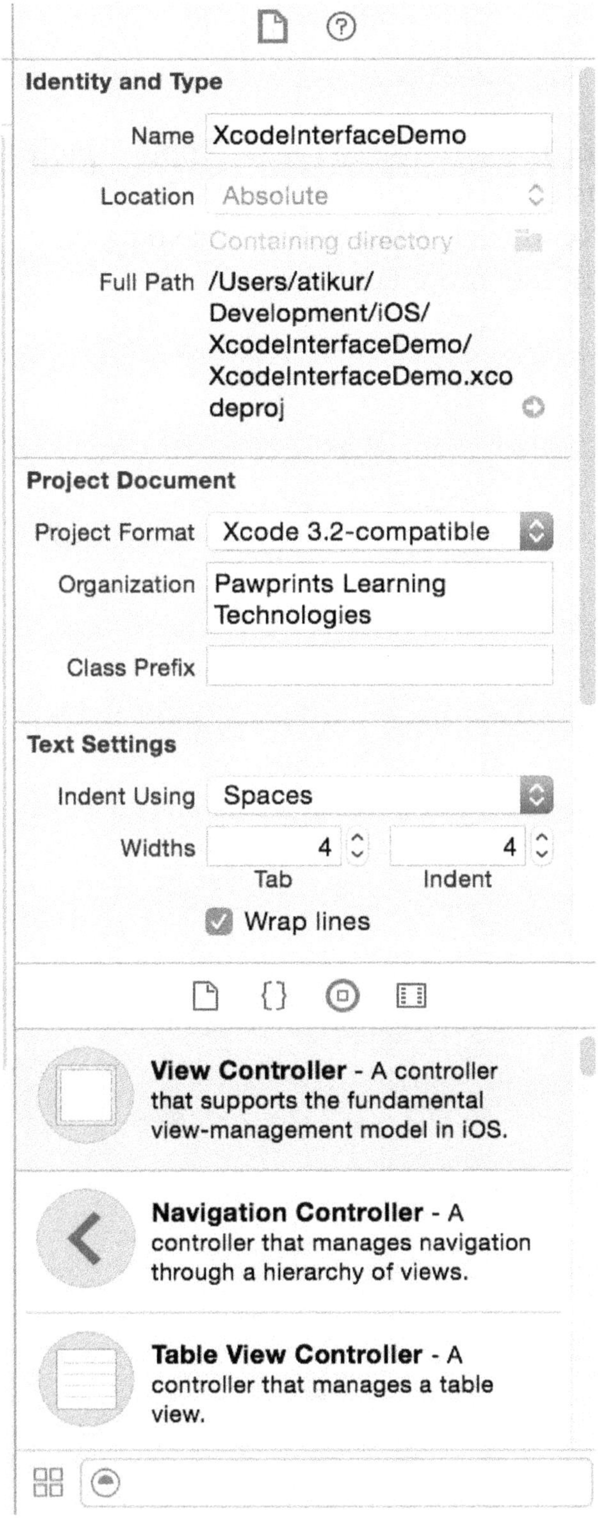

Identity and Type

Name XcodeInterfaceDemo

Location Absolute

Containing directory

Full Path /Users/atikur/
Development/iOS/
XcodeInterfaceDemo/
XcodeInterfaceDemo.xco
deproj

Project Document

Project Format Xcode 3.2-compatible

Organization Pawprints Learning
Technologies

Class Prefix

Text Settings

Indent Using Spaces

Widths 4 · 4 ·
 Tab Indent

☑ Wrap lines

View Controller - A controller
that supports the fundamental
view-management model in iOS.

Navigation Controller - A
controller that manages navigation
through a hierarchy of views.

Table View Controller - A
controller that manages a table
view.

Figure 1-10

17

Summary

This chapter introduced you to Xcode the tool you will use to create Apple Watch apps. Xcode is quite a complex tool, with lots of stuff included. So, don't feel discouraged if you aren't comfortable with Xcode yet. After you spend some time with Xcode and create more projects, you will feel more confident with it.

Chapter 2: Your First Apple Watch App

In this chapter, we will write our first Apple Watch app. Let's get started by opening Xcode.

Your First Watch App

In order to create an Apple Watch app, you must have an existing iOS app. So, create a new **Single View Application** by following these steps–

1. From the Xcode welcome screen, click "Create a New Xcode Project" (alternatively, you can click Xcode File Menu, *File -> New -> Project ...*).

2. Select "Single View Application" template (Figure 2-1).

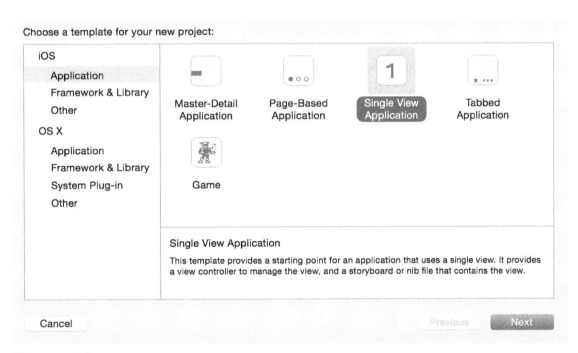

Figure 2-1

3. Enter "FirstWatchApp" as **Product Name**, *Swift* as **Language** and *iPhone* for **Devices** dropdown (Figure 2-2).

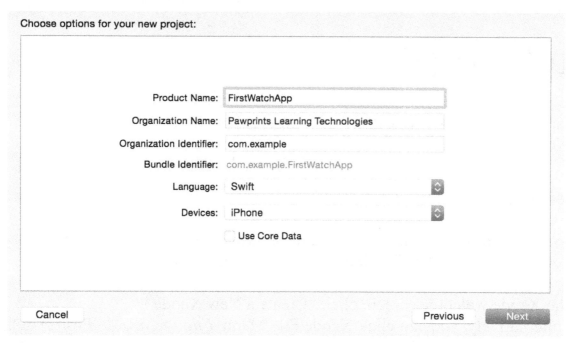

Figure 2-2

4. Click **Next** and then save the project to a convenient location.

At this stage, you have a simple iOS app (when we say 'iOS', we mean iPhone/iPad/etc) with an empty screen. You can run the iOS application by clicking the Run button from Xcode's toolbar. Go ahead and press the run button. You will see your application running on the iPhone simulator (Figure 2-3).

Figure 2-3

Congratulations for running your first iOS app successfully! In the next step, we will add Watch App support to our existing iOS app. Before you move on further, press the Stop button from Xcode toolbar to stop the running iOS app.

Adding WatchKit

You need to add a **Watch App** target to your iOS app.

1. Select your project in the Project Navigator and then click the + button at the bottom of the project/target pane (Figure 2-4).

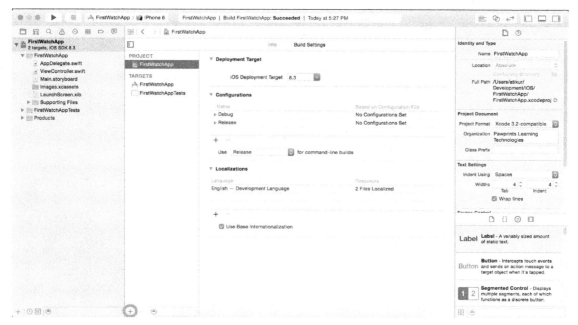

Figure 2-4

2. A new window will appear (Figure 2-5). From the left section of the window, select **Apple Watch** under the iOS group and then select **WatchKit App**. Click **Next**.

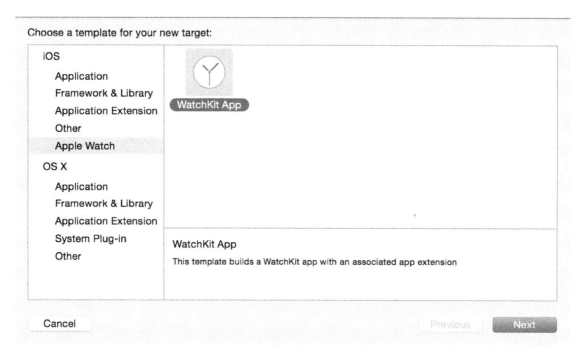

Figure 2-5

3. The next screen will let you choose options for your new target (Figure 2-6). Make sure your settings look similar to Figure 2-6.

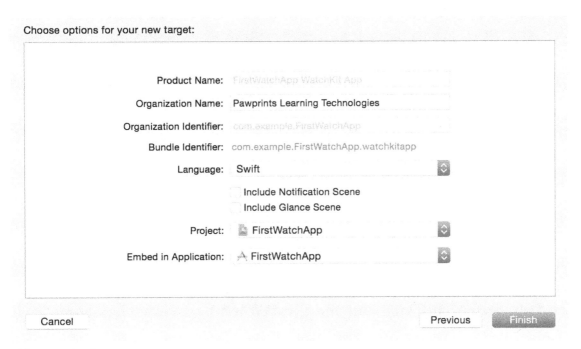

Figure 2-6

4. Click **Finish** when your settings look similar to Figure 2-6.

5. You might get a new window to confirm whether you would like to activate a new scheme for your WatchKit App target (Figure 2-7). Click **Activate**. This will add a new scheme for your Watchkit App. We will select this scheme from Xcode toolbar when we run the Watch app.

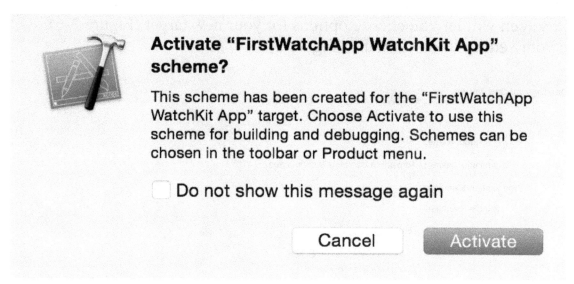

Figure 2-7

6. You will notice that there are two new folders in your project navigator:
FirstWatchApp WatchKit Extension and **FirstWatchApp WatchKit App**
(Figure 2-8).

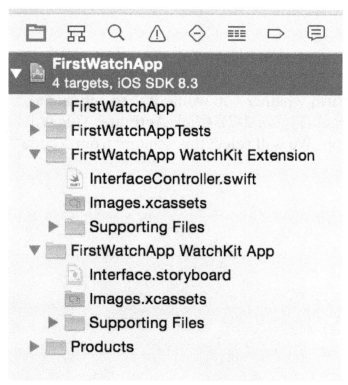

Figure 2-8

The WatchKit Extension will contain the logic and core functionality of your
Watch app (generally, the Swift code files). These code files won't run on Apple

Watch, instead they will run on the iPhone connected with the Apple Watch. On the other hand, the WatchKit App will contain resource files, these files will be actually hosted on the Apple Watch.

Running Watch App

From the scheme dropdown menu of the Xcode toolbar, select **FirstWatchApp WatchKit App -> iPhone 6** (Figure 2-9) and then hit the **run button**.

Figure 2-9

You should see two simulators, one for iPhone app and watch app. If you only see a iPhone simulator, from the simulator menu, go to **Hardware -> External Displays -> Apple Watch 38mm** (Figure 2-10).

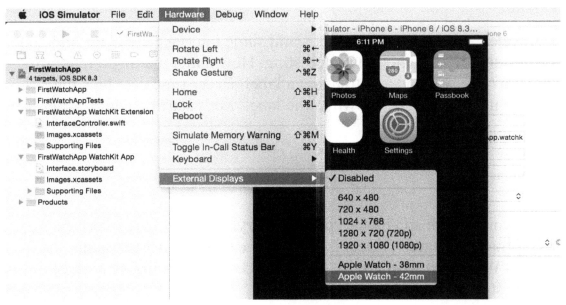

Figure 2-10

You should see the watch simulator now (Figure 2-11). Not very exciting yet, but we are certainly making some progress!

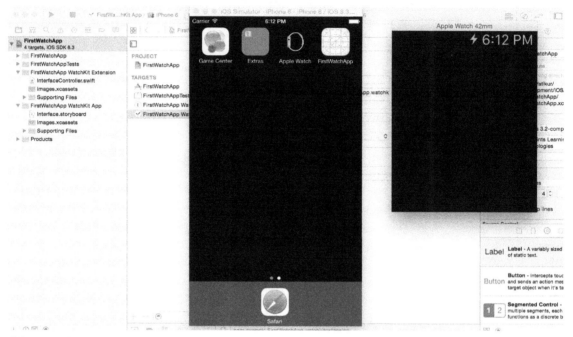

Figure 2-11

Random Number Generator App

Currently our watch app does nothing. Let's add some interface elements and code to our watch app so it does something interesting. How about making a random number generator? We will add a button and a label. Every time user taps the button, a random number will be shown in the label. Let's start by adding interface elements.

Add Interface Elements

You can design your Watch app interface using storyboards and the Interface Builder. From project navigator, select the **Interface.storyboard** file under the **FirstWatchApp WatchKit App** group. You will see a single empty Interface Controller in the storyboard (Figure 2-12).

Figure 2-12

Now, let's add some controls to it. Start by dragging a Button from the object library to the interface (Figure 2-13).

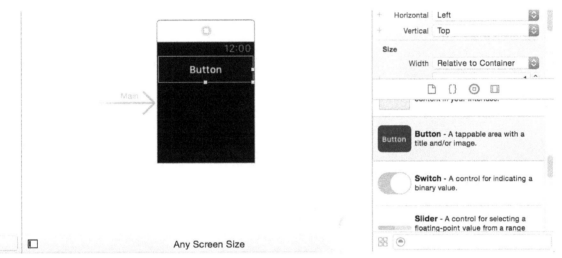

Figure 2-13

Let's change the button text. Double click on the button's text and change the text to "Generate" (Figure 2-14).

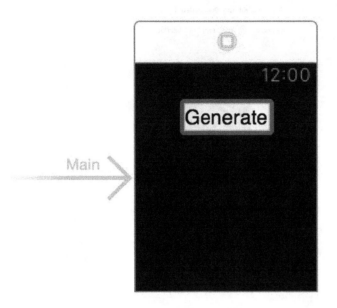

Figure 2-14

Next, drag a Label from object library and place it underneath the button (Figure 2-15).

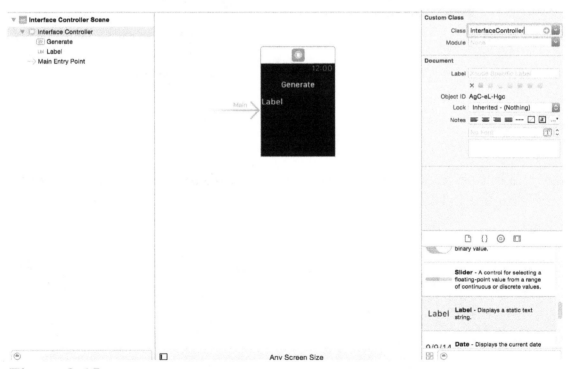

Figure 2-15

28

The interface design for our Random Number Generator app is complete. Let's add some code to make the app working.

Running Some Code

We need to run some code when the "Generate" button is tapped, so that a new random number is generated and shown to the label. But where should we put these code?

The code for our watch app should live in WatchKit Extension group. If you expand the **FirstWatchApp WatchKit Extension** group, you will see a Swift file named **InterfaceController.swift** (Figure 2-16). This is the code file associated with the interface controller of our storyboard. You can verify that by selecting the Interface.storyboard file and then select the Interface Controller icon (yellow icon at the top of interface controller). Then check the Identity Inspector (select third button of utility pane). Under the custom class, you will see **InterfaceController** as the value of **Class** field (Figure 2-17). This InterfaceController refers to the InterfaceController.swift file of the WatchKit Extension group.

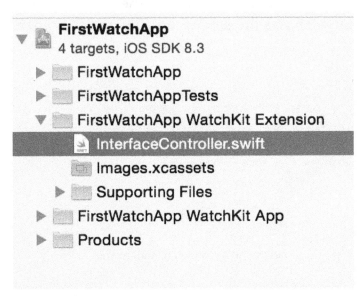

Figure 2-16

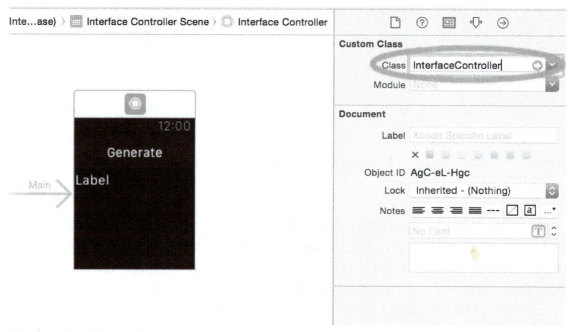

Figure 2-17

So, let's add some code that will run when the "Generate" button is tapped. Click the **Assistant Editor** button from the Xcode toolbar. You will see the editor pane is split into two windows, where one window shows the storyboard file and the other one shows the code file (Figure 2-18).

Figure 2-18

If Xcode doesn't show these two files, you can manually select them. First, select the Interface.storyboard file from the project navigator. Then, from the Xcode jump bar (where it says Automatic), select "Manual", browse through the project files and select InterfaceController.swift file (Figure 2-19).

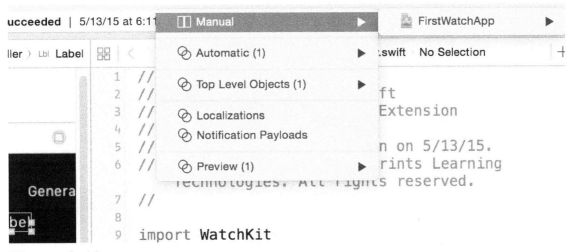

Figure 2-19

Now, Control-drag from the "Generate" button in Interface Builder to InterfaceController.swift file in the assistant editor. Xcode will indicate where you can insert an outlet or action in your code (Figure 2-20).

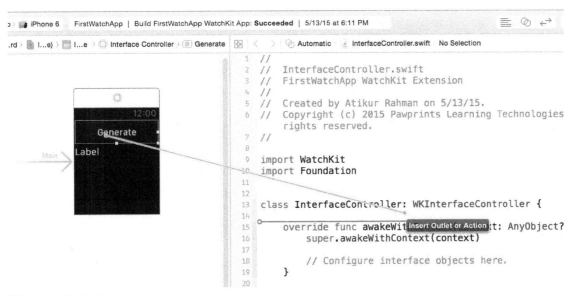

Figure 2-20

When you release the mouse button, the assistant editor displays a Connection menu (Figure 2-21).

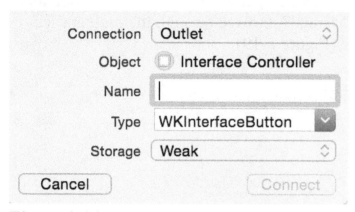

Figure 2-21

Select **Action** from the **Connection** dropdown. Enter "generateButtonTapped" as the value of **Name** field (Figure 2-22).

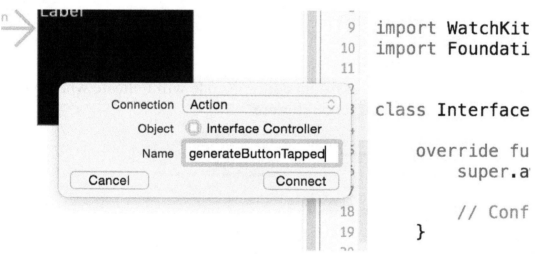

Figure 2-22

Finally, click **Connect**. This will add a new action **generateButtonTapped().** You can consider an action as a piece of code that runs when something happens (like user taps a button or change value of slider). Currently the action generateButtonTapped() is empty, we need to add code inside the curly braces that follow the action name.

```
import WatchKit
import Foundation


class InterfaceController: WKInterfaceController {

    @IBAction func generateButtonTapped() {
    }

    override func awakeWithContext(context: AnyObject
        super.awakeWithContext(context)

        // Configure interface objects here.
    }
```

Figure 2-23

Now, update the generateButtonTapped() action method with following code –

```
    @IBAction func generateButtonTapped() {
        let number = arc4random_uniform(100)
        println(number)
    }
```

The first line generates a random number between 0 to 99 and assigns that number to the constant named **number**. The second line prints the value of **number** to the console. Don't worry too much about the code right now, Chapter 3 will introduce you to the Swift language.

Now, if you run the watch app and click the "Generate" button, a new random number will be displayed to the console window of Xcode (figure 2-24).

Figure 2-24

33

So, congratulations for writing your first Swift code!

Now, let's display the random number to the Label. In order to access the Label from InterfaceController.swift file, we need to add an **Outlet**. An outlet is simply a connection that let us access a storyboard control from code. The process of adding an outlet is similar to the process of adding an action.

Control-drag from the Label in Interface Builder to InterfaceController.swift file in assistant editor. Release the mouse button, a connection menu will be displayed. Enter "numberLabel" as the value of **Name** field and keep other options unchanged (Figure 2-25).

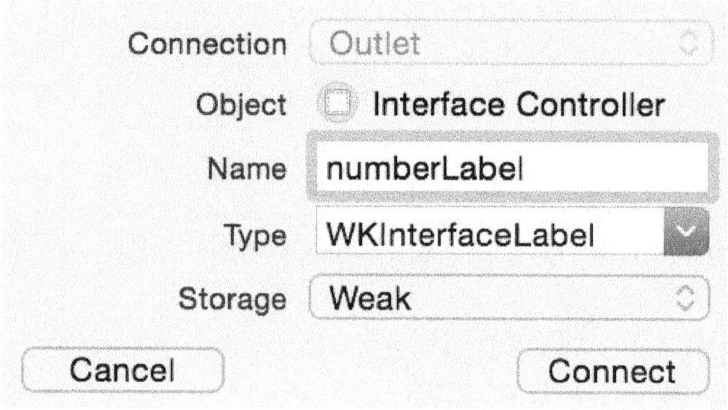

Connection	Outlet
Object	Interface Controller
Name	numberLabel
Type	WKInterfaceLabel
Storage	Weak
Cancel	Connect

Figure 2-25

Click **Connect**. Xcode will create a new outlet for the label (Figure 2-26).

```
import WatchKit
import Foundation


class InterfaceController: WKInterfaceController {

    @IBOutlet weak var numberLabel: WKInterfaceLabel!

    @IBAction func generateButtonTapped() {
        let number = arc4random_uniform(100)
        println(number)
    }
```

Figure 2-26

Now, update the generateButtonTapped() method as follows –

```
@IBAction func generateButtonTapped() {
    let number = arc4random_uniform(100)
    numberLabel.setText(String(number))
}
```

The second line of generateButtonTapped() method is updated. Instead of printing the random number to console output, now it sets the random number to the label using the setText() method of **numberLabel** outlet.

Now, run the watch app and tap the "Generate" button. A new random number will be displayed to the label (Figure 2-27).

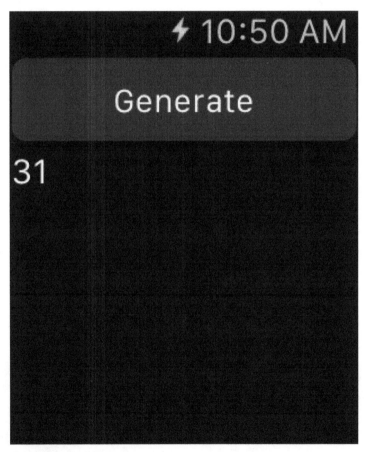

Figure 2-27

Every time you click the "Generate" button, a new number will be displayed to the label.

How it works?

When you tap "Generate" button, the generateButtonTapped() action is called.

```
let number = arc4random_uniform(100)
```

This line generates a random number between 0 to 99 and assigns that value to the constant named **number**. You will learn more about constants in the next chapter, for now just consider it as a container for some value.

```
numberLabel.setText(String(number))
```

This line updates the text of Label with the value stored in **number**.

Summary

Congratulations for your first working Watch App! You learned a lot in this chapter. You created an iOS app and then added Watch App support to it. You learned about actions and outlets. You even wrote couple of lines of Swift code! The next chapter will introduce you to the Swift language in much more detail.

Chapter 3: Introducing Swift

In this chapter, we learn about the Swift language. Swift is Apple's new programming language for Mac and iOS development. The Swift language is intended to be the future replacement of Objective-C, which was the only language available for developing Mac and iOS apps for many years.

Xcode Playground

We will use the Xcode playground to learn the Swift language. Playground allows us to write Swift code and see the results of each line of code in the sidebar immediately. It's a great way to learn the Swift language interactively.

Create a new Playground

You can create a new Playground from the Xcode welcome screen. Select "Get started with a playground" option to create a new playground (Figure 3-1).

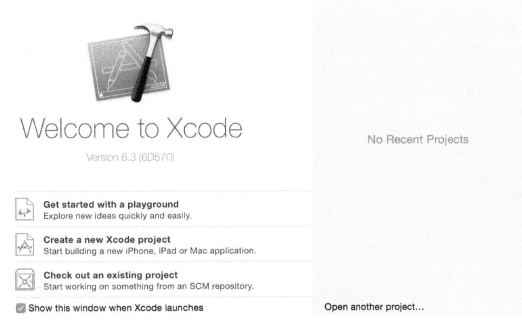

Figure 3-1

Alternatively, you can create a new playground from the Xcode File menu. Select -

File -> New -> Playground...

In either case, you will see a screen like Figure 3-2

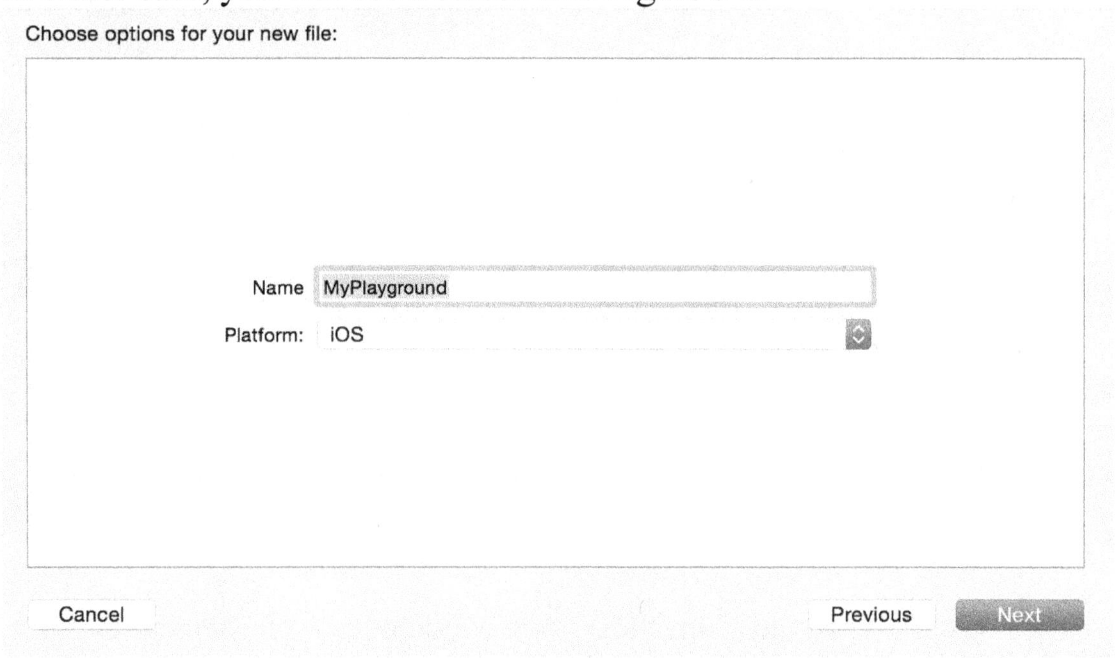

Choose options for your new file:

Name MyPlayground

Platform: iOS

Cancel   Previous   Next

Figure 3-2

Name the playground and set **Platform** to **iOS**. Click "Next" and tell Xcode where you'd like to save the playground. Click "Create" to finish the process. Instead of creating a full project with a bunch of files and folders, it will create a single file with a **.playground** extension (Figure 3-3).

```
                               MyPlayground.playground
      <    >      MyPlayground.playground
    1   //: Playground - noun: a place where people can play
    2
    3   import UIKit
    4
    5   var str = "Hello, playground"                          "Hello, playground"
    6
```

- 30 sec +

Figure 3-3

As you can see, the user interface of a playground is very simple. On the left, you see a code editor with a couple of lines of code and on the right, you see the output or results generated by the code on the left.

Let's take a moment to understand the default code generated in our playground file. The first line is a comment. Comments do not produce any output, they are notes for programmers. Any line of code that starts with two forward slashes (//) is a comment in Swift.

The second line is an import statement –

import UIKit

UIKit is a framework written by Apple Engineers, which consists of pre-written code to help you create user interface of your iOS applications. The above import statement gives you access to every class and constant declared in UIKit framework.

The third line declares a variable and assigns a value to that. You will learn more about variables in the next section.

Variables and Constants

Your app will often need to remember different things. For example, if you build a game, you will need to remember the player's score, number of enemies destroyed, weapons available and many other things. These things are generally referred to as data.

You can use variables to remember such things (or data). You can think of a variable as a temporary storage container for a single piece of data. For example, let's use a variable to store a player's score –

> var score = 90

The above statement declares a variable named **score**, which holds the value 90. Now, type the above statement to the playground. You will see the value 90 shown in the output area (right side of the editor). You can also add number with the variable **score** and do all sorts of arithmetic operations –

```
1  var score = 90                                          90
2  score + 15                                              105
```

Figure 3-4

As you can see, the playground evaluates the statements and shows the result immediately.

You will often need to replace value stored in a variable with a new value. For example, player's score doesn't stay same all the time –

```
1  var score = 90          90
2  score = 110             110
```

Figure 3-5

The second statement (Figure 3-5) will replace the old value of **score** with new value.

Data comes in all kinds of shapes and sizes. The good news is, there are containers of all sorts and sizes as well. Different types of variables hold different types of values. Variables can hold numbers, text strings, Boolean types (true/false) or even a custom data type.

The following playground file (Figure 3-6) shows some example of different types of variables -

```
1  // whole number (or integer)
2  var score = 90                              90
3
4  // floating point number (or float/double)
5  var price = 9.75                            9.75
6
7  // Boolean type
8  var isAllowed = true                        true
9
10 // string type
11 var name = "Kate"                           "Kate"
12
```

Figure 3-6

You might be wondering how Swift understands what type of variables to use for different types of data since you haven't explicitly set any types for these variables. The Swift compiler has enough information about the data being stored, so it automatically infers the right type.

For example, because you set **score** to 90, the Swift compiler knows 90 is an Integer, so it sets the type of **score** to an **Int** (data type of Integer numbers) automatically.

However, you can set the type explicitly if you want –

    var score: Int = 90

You tell the type of a variable by putting a colon after the variable name, followed by the type of the variable.

You may wonder if you should set types explicitly or let the compiler infer the types for you. In Swift, it's standard practice to let the compiler infer types automatically where possible, which makes the code concise and easy to read.

Swift is very strict about data type. Once you declare a variable as one type, you can't put value of any other type to that variable. For example, take a look at following code -

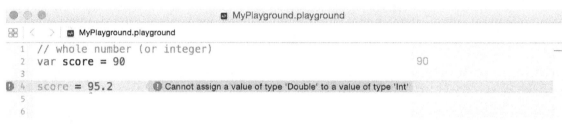

Figure 3-7

The **score** variable holds integer value. Later, when you try to replace the current value with a double (or number with decimal point) value, you get an error.

Constants

Some data must remain unchanged throughout the program. For example, you might need to remember a user's birthday in your program. For these situations, you should use a **constant** instead of a variable. Once the value of a constant is set, it never changes for it's entire lifetime. If you attempt to change value of a constant, you will get an error.

Creating a constant is very similar to creating a variable. The only difference is that instead of using *var*, you use the keyword **let** to declare a constant.

Figure 3-8

Data Types

In this section, we will briefly discuss about different data types available in Swift.

Int (Integer)

An integer is a whole number, which is simply a number without any decimal places. It can be positive or negative. For example –

Figure 3-9

Float

In Swift, you can have numeric values with decimal places. For example, you might need to represent price of a product. A decimal-based numeric value is called a floating point (or float).

```
1  // Float
2
3  var x: Float = 5.9        5.9
4  var y = -10.3             -10.3
5
```

Figure 3-10

Bool (Boolean)

Booleans are represented by the *Bool* type, which has one of two possible values – true or false.

```
                          MyPlayground.playground
      <  >    MyPlayground.playground
 1  // Boolean
 2
 3  var x = true                                    true
 4  var y: Bool = false                             false
 5
```

Figure 3-11

String

A string is a bunch of characters surrounded by a pair of quotes. It consists of a series of letters, numbers and symbols.

```
                          MyPlayground.playground
      <  >    MyPlayground.playground
 1  // String
 2
 3  var name = "John"                               "John"
 4  var message: String = "Hello"                   "Hello"
 5
```

Figure 3-12

Arrays

Suppose you need to store the name of each student of a class. You could create a variable for each student. But for 50 students, you would need to create 50 different variables. As you can see, that would get cumbersome. To solve problems like this, you could use an array.

An array is a group of items placed in a specific order. Each item of array can be accessed via an index. The index is a number that indicates the position of that particular item inside the array. You can create an array like this –

```
var names = ["James", "Kate", "Mike", "Andy", "Sara"]
```

You start with the **var** keyword, followed by the name of the array. On the other side of the 'equals' sign, you put the items of your array inside brackets separated by a comma.

Arrays must all have the same type of data. The above example array holds string type data. Similarly, you can create array of integers or floats, but you can't have an array that holds a mixture of integers and floats.

Like normal variables, Swift can infer the type automatically for a given array. But if your array has different type of items, the Swift compiler will return an error. You have the option to explicitly declare the type of array, this is how you can do that -

```
var names: [String] = ["James", "Kate", "Mike", "Andy", "Sara"]
```

Again, this is similar to type declaration of a normal variable, the only difference is you put the array type inside brackets.

Accessing Array Items

You use index to access an array item, where index is a number that indicates the position of that particular item inside the array. Indexes always start with zero. So, the first item in the array will be at index 0, the second item in the array is at index 1, the third item in the array is at index 2 and so on. Here is how you access an item inside an array —

```
1  var names = ["James", "Kate", "Mike",      ["James", "Kate", "Mike", "Andy", "Sara"]
       "Andy", "Sara"]
2
3  names[0]                                    "James"
4  names[1]                                    "Kate"
5  names[2]                                    "Mike"
```

Figure 3-13

The format to access an array item is, you put index inside brackets after the array name.

To get the first item and last item of an array, you can use the **first** and **last** property respectively –

```
1   var names = ["James", "Kate", "Mike",          ["James", "Kate", "Mike", "Andy", "Sara"]
        "Andy", "Sara"]
2
3   names.first                                      "James"
4   names.last                                       "Sara"
```

Figure 3-14

You can use **count** property to get the total number of items in the array –

```
1   var names = ["James", "Kate", "Mike",          ["James", "Kate", "Mike", "Andy", "Sara"]
        "Andy", "Sara"]
2
3   names.count                                      5
```

Figure 3-15

To check if an array is empty or not, you can use **isEmpty** property –

```
1   var names = ["James", "Kate", "Mike",          ["James", "Kate", "Mike", "Andy", "Sara"]
        "Andy", "Sara"]
2
3   names.isEmpty                                    false
```

Figure 3-16

Modifying arrays

Arrays declared with **var** keyword are mutable and can be changed as needed (you can declare immutable arrays using **let** keyword). Array data type has a number of methods to help you modify its items.

To add an item to the end of your array, you can use the append() method –

```
1   var names = ["James", "Kate", "Mike"]          ["James", "Kate", "Mike"]
2
3   names.append("Alice")                           ["James", "Kate", "Mike", "Alice"]
4
```

Figure 3-17

You can replace an item in the array with a new item by accessing its index and setting it to a new value –

```
1   var names = ["James", "Kate", "Mike"]     ["James", "Kate", "Mike"]
2
3   names[1] = "Alice"                          "Alice"
4
5   names                                       ["James", "Alice", "Mike"]
```

Figure 3-18

The insert() method can be used to insert an item at a specific location –

```
1   var names = ["James", "Kate", "Mike"]       ["James", "Kate", "Mike"]
2
3   names.insert("Bob", atIndex: 2)             ["James", "Kate", "Bob", "Mike"]
```

Figure 3-19

To remove an item from a specific index, you can use removeAtIndex() method –

```
1   var names = ["James", "Kate", "Mike"]       ["James", "Kate", "Mike"]
2
3   names.removeAtIndex(1)                       "Kate"
4
5   names                                        ["James", "Mike"]
```

Figure 3-20

Dictionaries

Dictionaries can store multiple values that are uniquely associated with keys. Items of a dictionary are not organized in a specific order. You use the key to store or look up a value. Take a look at an example dictionary –

```
var students = ["Sarah": 13, "Bob": 10, "Kate": 12]
```

The above example declares a dictionary with three items (key-value pairs) and assigns the dictionary to a variable named *students*. Each item (key-value pair) of dictionary follows the syntax –

key: value

You enclose the items with brackets, where each item is comma separated.

47

All keys of a dictionary must be of same data type and all values must be of same data type as well. You can explicitly declare type as follows –

```
var students: [String: Int] = ["Sarah": 13, "Bob": 10, "Kate": 12]
```

In case you explicitly specify the data type of dictionary, you need to specify data type for both keys and values.

To access the value of an item of dictionary, you provide corresponding key inside the brackets –

```
1  var students = ["Sarah": 13, "Bob": 10,      ["Bob": 10, "Sarah": 13, "Kate": 12]
       "Kate": 12]
2
3  students["Bob"]                               10
```

Figure 3-21

You can add another key-value pair as follows –

```
1  var students = ["Sarah": 13, "Bob": 10,      ["Bob": 10, "Sarah": 13, "Kate": 12]
       "Kate": 12]
2
3  students["Jack"] = 11                         11
4
5  students                                      ["Sarah": 13, "Bob": 10, "Kate": 12, "Jack": 11]
```

Figure 3-22

To replace an item's value, you need to set a new value for that key –

```
1  var students = ["Sarah": 13, "Bob": 10,      ["Bob": 10, "Sarah": 13, "Kate": 12]
       "Kate": 12]
2
3  students["Bob"] = 15                          15
4
5  students                                      ["Bob": 15, "Sarah": 13, "Kate": 12]
```

Figure 3-23

To remove a key-value pair, you need to set the value *nil* for that key –

```
1  var students = ["Sarah": 13, "Bob": 10,      ["Bob": 10, "Sarah": 13, "Kate": 12]
       "Kate": 12]
2
3  students["Bob"] = nil                         nil
4
5  students                                      ["Kate": 12, "Sarah": 13]
```

Figure 3-24

In Swift, *nil* means no value.

If Statements

While writing code, sometimes you will want to run some code only if some conditions are met. You can use *if* statement to do that. For example –

```
     MyPlayground.playground
1  var productPrice = 45                             45
2  var availableBalance = 110                        110
3
4  if productPrice <= availableBalance {
5      println("Eligible to buy the product")        "Eligible to buy the product"
6  }
```

Figure 3-25

The above *if* statement checks whether the *productPrice* is less than or equal to *availableBalance*. If that condition is true, only then the code associated with that *if* statement will run (code inside curly braces). For the above example, since the condition is true, the code inside the curly braces will run.

In case of the *if* statement, you start with the *if* keyword, followed by the condition in question and finally you put a block of code inside curly braces. This code block runs only if the condition is true, otherwise the code block will be ignored.

The *if* statement can have an alternative set of statements, known as an *else clause*, which run when the *if* condition is false. For example –

```
     MyPlayground.playground
1  var productPrice = 45                                      45
2  var availableBalance = 20                                  20
3
4  if productPrice <= availableBalance {
5      println("Eligible to buy the product")
6  } else {
7      println("Not enough balance to purchase the product")  "Not enough balance to purchase the product"
8  }
```

Figure 3-26

In the above example, since the condition of *if* statement is false, the *else* block will be executed.

For Loops

In our app, sometimes we need to execute a set of statements a certain number of times. Swift provides two variants of *for* loop –

- The *for-in* loop, which allows us to execute a set of statements for each item in a sequence.
- The *for* loop, which is good for executing a set of statements until a specific condition is met.

The for Loop

You can use *for* loop to execute a set of statements until a specified condition is met. It has the following syntax –

```
for initialization; condition; increment {
    statements
}
```

Here is an example for loop, which prints the numbers 0 to 9 –

```
for var i = 0; i < 10; i++ {
    println(i)
}
```

As you can see, the *for* loop definition has three parts – *initialization, condition* and *increment*. Each of these three parts are separated using semicolons.

Here is how a *for* loop is executed –

1. At the beginning of the loop, the *initialization* expression is evaluated once. Here you set up any variables or constants that are needed for the loop.

2. The *condition* expression is evaluated, if it evaluates to *true*, statements inside the braces are executed. If the *condition* expression evaluates to *false*, the loop ends and code execution continues after the *for* loop's closing brace (*}*).

3. After all the statements within the braces are executed, the *increment* expression is evaluated. Here you will typically increase or decrease the value of a counter.

After the execution of *increment* expression, execution returns to step 2 and the *condition* expression is evaluated again.

The for-in Loop

The *for-in* loop can be used to iterate over a sequence, such as ranges of numbers, items in an array or characters in a string.

The general syntax of *for-in* loop is –

```
for index in sequence {
    statements
}
```

Where, *index* is a constant whose value is automatically set at the start of each iteration of the loop. For the first iteration of the loop, the value of *index* will be the first item of the sequence, for second iteration of loop, the value of *index* will be the second item of the sequence and so on.

Let's consider the following array –

```
var names = ["Alice", "Bob", "John", "Mike"]
```

We can use *for-in* loop to iterate through the items of the above array as follows –

```
for name in names {
    println(name)
}
```

In each iteration of the *for-in* loop, an item of the array is assigned to the variable *name* and statements inside the curly braces are executed. In this case, there is a single statement inside the braces, but it can contain multiple statements.

The While loop

A *while* loop can be used to perform a set of statements until a condition becomes *false*. These types of loops are best suited for situations where the number of iterations is unknown before the first iteration begins.

The general form of a while loop is –

```
while condition {
    statements
}
```

The *condition* is evaluated at the start of each pass through the loop, as long as it evaluates to *true*, the statements inside the braces are executed. When the *condition* becomes *false*, the *while* loop execution ends.

Here is an example of a while loop –

```
var i = 0

while i < 10 {
    println(i)
    i++
}
```

In the above example, we have a variable *i*, which has initial value of 0. The *while* loop checks whether the value of *i* is less than 10 or not. If the condition is *true*, the statements inside the braces are executed (prints the current value of *i* and increments the current value of *i* by 1). After the statements inside the braces are executed, the loop condition is checked again and loop execution continues as long as the condition evaluates to *true*. At one stage, the loop condition evaluates to *false* (when *i* equals to 10) and then the *while* loop execution stops. As a result, the above *while* loop will print numbers from 0 to 9.

Example: Prime Number Checker

We learned various building blocks of Swift language, like variables, conditional statements (e.g. if statement), looping statements(e.g. for loop, while loop etc). In this section, we will write a simple program which uses various Swift programming concepts we learned in previous sections of this chapter. We will write a program which can tell whether a given number is prime or not.

A prime number is a natural number greater than 1, that has no positive divisors other than 1 and itself. Some example prime numbers are 2, 3, 5, 7, 11 etc.

1. Create a new playground file named *PrimeCheker.playground* by selecting the Xcode menu item -

    File -> New -> Playground...

2. Update the *PrimerChecker.playground* file with the following code (Figure 3-27) –

```
   PrimeChecker.playground
1  var number = 21                                              21
2  var isPrime = true                                           true
3
4  for i in 2..<number {
5      if number % i == 0 {
6          isPrime = false                                      false
7          break
8      }
9  }
10
11 println("\(number) is a prime: \(isPrime)")                  "21 is a prime: false"
```

Figure 3-27

3. The above example checks whether 21 is a prime or not. Since 21 has positive divisors other than 1 and itself (e.g. 3 and 7), it is not a prime number. The above program also detects that 21 is not a prime, as you can see the output of line 11 (Figure 3-27), which says -

    21 is a prime: false

4. Change the value of the variable *number* to some other integer value and check the output.

How it works?

To check whether a number is prime or not, we need to see if that number has any positive divisor other than 1 and itself. We declare a Boolean variable *isPrime*, with initial value set to *true* –

    var **isPrime** = true

Then we use *for-in* loop to loop through the sequence of numbers from 2 to one less than the value stored in the variable *number*.

```
for i in 2..<number {

}
```

The above operator **..<** generates a sequence of numbers from 2 to one less than the value stored in the variable *number*. So if the value of the variable *number* is 21, then –

```
2..<21
```

will generate a sequence of numbers from 2 to 20.

For each iteration of the above *for-in* loop, the variable *i* will be assigned to a number of that sequence and the following statements will be executed –

```
if number % i == 0 {
    isPrime = false
    break
}
```

Here, we check whether *i* is a divisor of *number* or not. In case *i* is a divisor of *number*, then *number* has a divisor other than 1 and itself. In that case, *number* isn't a prime and we set *isPrime* to *false*. Notice the *break* statement, which is used to end a loop.

Finally, the following statement prints the result of our program -

```
println("\(number) is a prime: \(isPrime)")
```

Notice the \() syntax here, which can be used to insert the value of a constant, variable or expression within a string. So, the above statement will replace the variables *number* and *isPrime* with their corresponding values and construct a string like following -

```
21 is a prime: false
```

Note: the above program to check prime number isn't efficient, rather it was kept simple for easy demonstration purpose. It also assumes that the value of the variable *number* is always greater than or equal to 2.

Summary

In this chapter, we learned how to test our code straightaway using the playground function in Xcode. We learnt about several Swift programming basics like variables, constants, and variable types. We learnt how to manipulate arrays and dictionaries. We learnt about if statements, and the while and for loops. We ended with a Prime Number checker to tie all the concepts together. These are valuable programming concepts that you should learn well for it will serve you well in the future.

In the next chapter, we will go back to Apple Watch development, working with images in our watch app.

Chapter 4: Working With Images

In this chapter, we will learn how to work with images. We will add images to our Watch App and learn how to change different attributes. We will also learn how to animate images.

Add an Image

In this section, we will see how to add an image to our Watch App. Let's start by creating an example Watch App –

1. Create an iOS app using **Single View Application** template and name it "ImageExamples". Make sure you select **Swift** as **Language** and **iPhone** as **Device**.

2. Now you need to add Watch App target to your iOS app. Select the project file in project navigator and click the + button at the bottom of project/target pane. A new window will appear, select **iOS -> Apple Watch -> WatchKit App** and click **Next**. The next screen let's you configure options for your new target. Configure options for your new target similar to Figure 4-1 and click **Finish**.

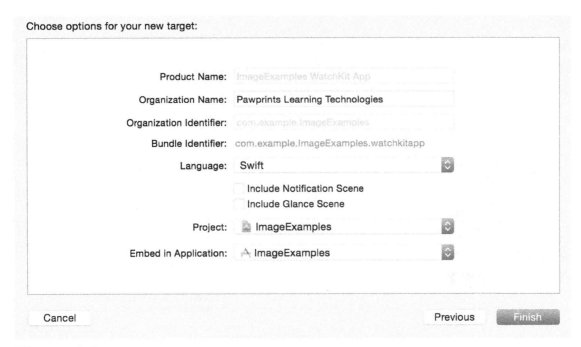

Choose options for your new target:

Product Name: ImageExamples WatchKit App

Organization Name: Pawprints Learning Technologies

Organization Identifier: com.example.ImageExamples

Bundle Identifier: com.example.ImageExamples.watchkitapp

Language: Swift

Include Notification Scene
Include Glance Scene

Project: ImageExamples

Embed in Application: ImageExamples

Cancel   Previous   Finish

Figure 4-1

3. You will notice two new groups added to your project navigator: **Image Examples WatchKit Extension** and **ImageExamples WatchKit App** (Figure 4-2).

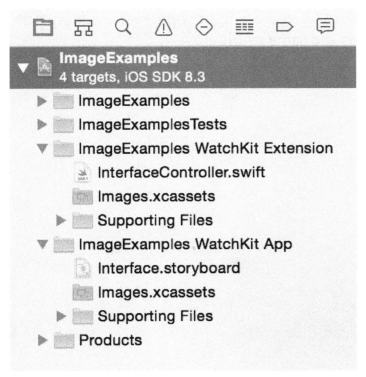

ImageExamples
4 targets, iOS SDK 8.3

▶ ImageExamples
▶ ImageExamplesTests
▼ ImageExamples WatchKit Extension
    InterfaceController.swift
    Images.xcassets
  ▶ Supporting Files
▼ ImageExamples WatchKit App
    Interface.storyboard
    Images.xcassets
  ▶ Supporting Files
▶ Products

Figure 4-2

4. Select *Interface.storyboard* file from the project navigator and drag an **Image** object from object library to the interface (Figure 4-3).

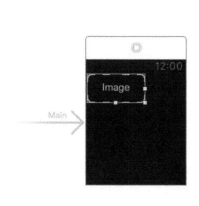

Figure 4-3

5. Now you need an actual image. This book comes with a downloadable archive, containing source code and other assets (including sample images). Open chapter 4 resources in Finder and drag the **car.png** file into the **ImageExamples WatchKit App** group. A new window will appear to let you configure options for adding new file. Make sure the options look exactly the same as Figure 4-4.

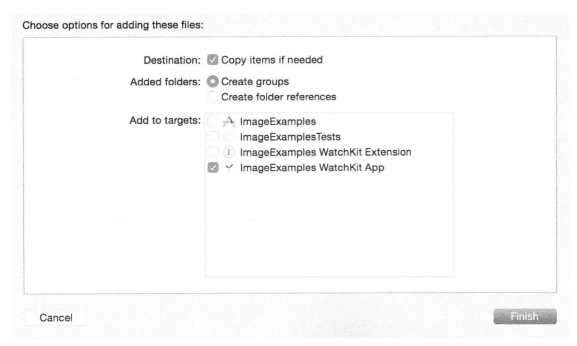

Figure 4-4

It's important that the options look exactly the same as Figure 4-4, especially **ImageExamples WatchKit App** and **Copy items if needed** must be checked.

6. Click **Finish** button. The **car.png** image will be added to the **ImageExamples WatchKit App** target (Figure 4-5).

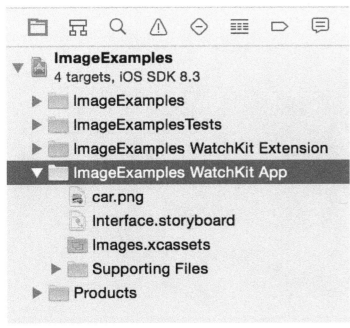

Figure 4-5

7. Now select the Image object in storyboard and go to **Attributes Inspector** (second last button of utility pane). Select **car.png** from the **Image** dropdown (Figure 4-6).

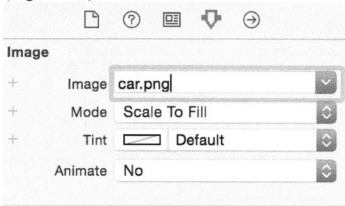

Figure 4-6

8. Once you select the car.png for **Image** attribute, it will be shown in the Image object in storyboard (Figure 4-7). You can change the size of the image by dragging the resize handle.

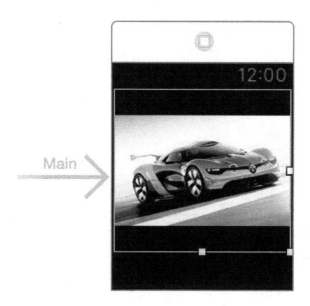

Figure 4-7

9. Run the Watch App and you should see something similar to Figure 4-8.

Figure 4-8

Manipulating Image

In this section, we will learn how to manipulate different attributes of image object.

Image Mode Attribute

The **Mode** attribute of an image object (Figure 4-9) determines how the actual image will be scaled to match the size. In this section, we will learn about some commonly used Mode values.

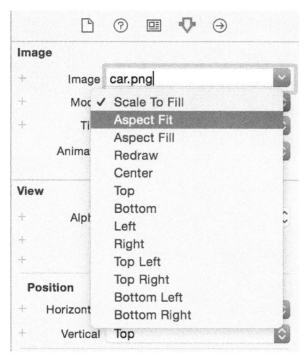

Figure 4-9

Scale To Fill

This is the default value of Mode attribute. This will fill the entire size of image object by scaling the image, without consideration to the ratio of width to height. As a result, if the size available for image object isn't the same as actual image size, you might get a distorted image.

Aspect Fit

The Aspect Fit mode will scale the image to fill the image object size, while maintaining the aspect ratio of the image. But there may be some letterboxing if the hosting image object's aspect ratio is different. This is the mode you will be using in most of the cases.

Aspect Fill

This mode will scale the image to fill the image object size, while maintaining the aspect ratio of the image. But there may be some cropping if the hosting image object's aspect ratio is different.

Change Image Size From Code

In most cases, you will change image size from storyboard just by dragging the resize handles or by changing width and height attributes. But, sometimes you might need to change those attributes from code. It's not that hard. Follow these steps –

1. Drag a Button from Object Library into storyboard and place it under the image. Rename the button text to "Resize" (4-10).

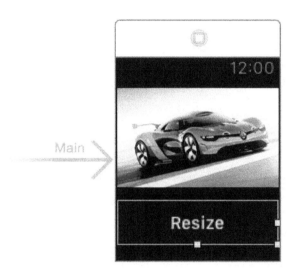

Figure 4-10

2. Click the Assistant Editor button and make sure the *Interface.storyboard* is displayed in the main editor window and *InterfaceController.swift* is displayed in the assistant editor window.

3. Add an **Outlet** for image by Ctrl-drag from image in storyboard to *InterfaceController.swift* file in assistant editor. Set the **Name** field as **carImage** (Figure 4-11).

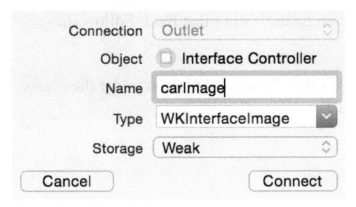

Figure 4-11

4. Add an Action for the button by Ctrl-drag from button in storyboard to *InterfaceController.swift* file in assistant editor. Set the **Name** field as **resizeButtonTapped** (Figure 4-12).

Figure 4-12

5. Update the resizeButtonTapped() action method with following code –

```
@IBAction func resizeButtonTapped() {
    carImage.setHeight(50)
}
```

6. Run the app using Watch App simulator. You should see an image and button similar to Figure 4-13.

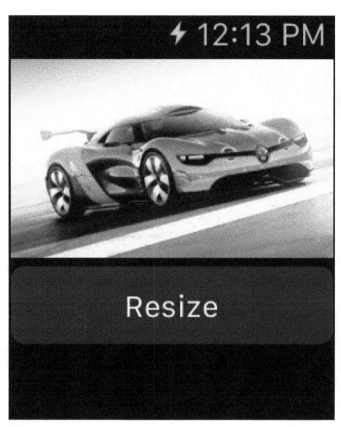

Figure 4-13

7. Now, tap on Resize button, the image size will be changed (Figure 4-14).

Figure 4-14

How it works?

When you tap the resize button, the `resizeButtonTapped()` method is called —

    carImage.setHeight(50)

The setHeight() method sets the height of image to 50 points. As a result, the image size changes.

Other Methods of WKInterfaceImage

The Image object (WKInterfaceImage) has other methods. You can change the width of by calling setWidth() method -

    carImage.setWidth(75)

The setImageNamed() method can be used to change the current image with a new one -

```
carImage.setImageNamed("car2.png")
```

The above line will replace the current image with another image named *car2.png*.

Animating Images

In this section, we will learn how to animate images.

1. Create a new iOS Single View app named *AnimatingImages*. Make sure you select *Swift* as **Language** and *iPhone* as **Device**.

2. Add Watch App target to your iOS app. If you don't remember how to do that, you can check previous examples.

3. Select *Interface.storyboard* file from *AnimatingImages WatchKit App* group.

4. Drag an Image object from Object library into your storyboard file. Use the resize handle of image object to resize the image size (Figure 4-15).

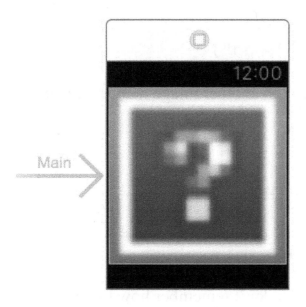

Figure 15

5. From Chapter 4 resources (which is part of downloadable archive that comes with this book), drag the images directory into *AnimatingImages WatchKit App* group. Make sure you configure the options similar to Figure 4-16.

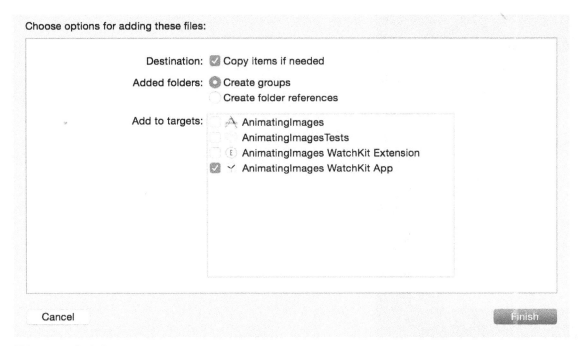

Figure 4-16

6. Select Image object from storyboard and change the below attributes from Attributes Inspector. Set value of **Image** attribute to *dancing*, **Mode** to *Aspect Fit*, **Animate** to *Yes* and **Duration** to *2*. Make sure the settings look similar to Figure 4-17.

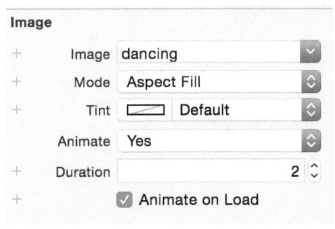

Figure 4-17

7. Run the Watch app (make sure you select WatchKit App scheme). When the app runs, you should see animating images (Figure 4-18).

Figure 4-18

How it works?

In order to animate images, we need a set of images, where each image will work as an individual frame. The images should have the same name, but with different frame numbers at the end. Here is how we named our images –

Figure 4-19

In this case, image name is *dancing* and the numbers at the end refers to the frame number. We also need to set the **Animate** property to *Yes*.

If you have a look at Attributes inspector (Figure 4-18), you will see that **Animate on Load** property is *checked*, which indicates that, images will start animating as soon as the storyboard is loaded.

Add a Button to Stop Animation

1. Select *Interface.storyboard* file. Resize the image object to make it a bit smaller and then drag a button below the image. Rename the button label to "Stop Animation" (Figure 4-20).

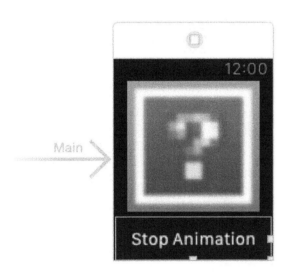

Figure 4-20

2. Add an **Outlet** for image by Ctrl-drag from image in storyboard to *InterfaceController.swift* file in assistant editor. Set the **Name** field as **danceImage**.

3. Add an Action for the button by Ctrl-drag from button in storyboard to *InterfaceController.swift* file in assistant editor. Set the **Name** field as **stopAnimationButtonTapped.**

71

4. Update the stopAnimationButtonTapped() action method with the following code –

```
@IBAction func stopAnimationButtonTapped() {
    danceImage.stopAnimating()
}
```

5. Run the Watch app again. You will see images animate when the app starts. If you click the "Stop Animation" button, the animation will stop immediately (Figure 4-21).

Figure 4-21

How it works?

We declared an outlet named **danceImage**, which refers to the image object in the storyboard. When the "Stop Animation" button is tapped, the action method stopAnimationButtonTapped() is called –

72

```
@IBAction func stopAnimationButtonTapped() {
    danceImage.stopAnimating()
}
```

The stopAnimating() method of image object stops the animation.

Similarly, the image object has another method called startAnimating(), which can be used to start animation.

Demo App: PhotoViewer

In this section, we will build an app called **PhotoViewer**. Every time the app is opened, it will show a random photo. The app will also contain a button. When the user taps that button, a new random photo will be shown.

1. Create a new iOS Single View app named *PhotoViewer*. Make sure you select *Swift* as **Language** and *iPhone* as **Device**.

2. Next, you need to add the Watch App target to your iOS app. Select the project file in project navigator and click the + button at the bottom of the project/target pane. A new window will appear. Select **iOS -> Apple Watch -> WatchKit App** and click **Next**. The next screen let's you configure options for your new target. Configure the options and click **Finish**.

3. From Chapter 4 resources, drag 5 images (image1.png, image2.png, image3.png, image4.png, image5.png) into *PhotoViewer WatchKit App* group. Make sure you configure the options similar to Figure 4-22.

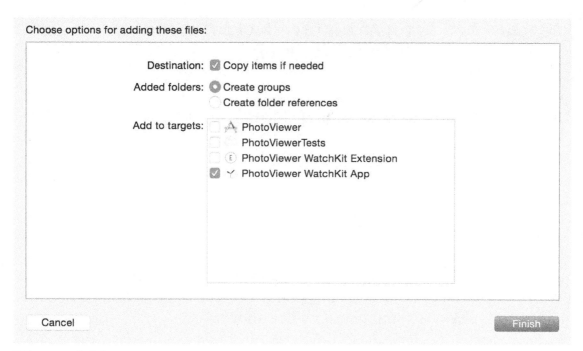

Choose options for adding these files:

Destination: ☑ Copy items if needed

Added folders: ⊙ Create groups
⃝ Create folder references

Add to targets:
☐ 🄰 PhotoViewer
☐ PhotoViewerTests
☐ Ⓔ PhotoViewer WatchKit Extension
☑ ⅄ PhotoViewer WatchKit App

Cancel   Finish

Figure 4-22

4. Select *Interface.storyboard* file from *PhotoViewr WatchKit App* group.

5. Drag an Image object from Object library into your storyboard file. Use the resize handle of image object to resize the image size (Figure 4-23). From Attributes Inspector, set the **Mode** attribute of Image object to "Aspect Fit".

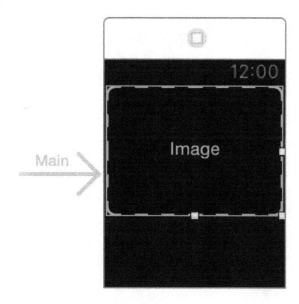

Figure 4-23

74

6. Drag a Button from Object Library into storyboard and place it under the image. Rename the button text to "Next Photo" (4-24).

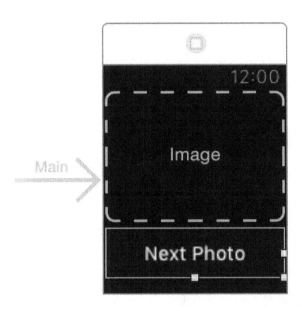

Figure 4-24

7. Click the Assistant Editor button and make sure the *Interface.storyboard* is displayed in mainhe editor window and *InterfaceController.swift* is displayed in the assistant editor window.

8. Add an **Outlet** for the image by Ctrl-drag from image in storyboard to *InterfaceController.swift* file in the assistant editor. Set the **Name** field as **myImage**.

9. Add an Action for the button by Ctrl-drag from the button in storyboard to *InterfaceController.swift* file in the assistant editor. Set the **Name** field as **nextPhotoButtonTapped**.

10. Next click the Standard Editor button and select *InterfaceController.swift* file. After the first opening curly brace ({), add the following line –

```
var images = ["image1.png", "image2.png", "image3.png", "image4.png",
    "image5.png"]
```

11. Update awakeWithContext() method with the following code -

```
override func awakeWithContext(context: AnyObject?) {
    super.awakeWithContext(context)

    var randomIndex =
Int(arc4random_uniform(UInt32(images.count)))
        myImage.setImageNamed(images[randomIndex])
    }
```

12. Update nextPhotoButtonTapped() action method with the following code –

```
@IBAction func nextPhotoButtonTapped() {
    var randomIndex =
Int(arc4random_uniform(UInt32(images.count)))
        myImage.setImageNamed(images[randomIndex])
    }
```

13. Save changes and run the Watch App. You will see a random image shown (Figure 4-25).

Figure 4-25

Tap the "Next Photo" button, you will get another random image.

How it works?

We declared an array named **images** with the image file names -

```
var images = ["image1.png", "image2.png", "image3.png", "image4.png",
    "image5.png"]
```

The **awakeWithContext()** method is called every time the app launches. Within this method, we added the following two lines of code –

```
var randomIndex = Int(arc4random_uniform(UInt32(images.count)))
myImage.setImageNamed(images[randomIndex])
```

The first line generates a random number between 0 and 4. The second line uses that random index to get a random image file name and sets that image to the outlet named *myImage*. Since awakeWithContext() method is called every time the app launches, the above two lines are called and a random image is set to *myImage*.

When the user taps "Next Photo" button, the following action method is called -

```
@IBAction func nextPhotoButtonTapped() {
    var randomIndex =
Int(arc4random_uniform(UInt32(images.count)))
    myImage.setImageNamed(images[randomIndex])
}
```

This action method contains exactly same two lines of code that we previously put to awakeWithContext() method. So, when user taps "Next Photo" button, a random photo is set to *myImage*.

Summary

In this chapter, we learnt how to add and manipulate images in our Watch app. We went on to illustrate how to animate images. We finally ended with a PhotoViewer app example.

Let's go on to the next chapter where we will explore working with Audio in our app.

Chapter 5: Working With Audio

In this chapter, we will learn how to work with audio in our Watch apps. We will add audio files and learn how to control audio playback. We will also learn how to control volume.

Play Audio

In this section, we will see how to play an audio file from our Watch App. Let's start by creating an example Watch App –

1. Create an iOS app using **Single View Application** template and name it "AudioExamples". Make sure you select **Swift** as **Language** and **iPhone** as **Device**.

2. Next, you need to add Watch App target to your iOS app. Select the project file in project navigator and click the + button at the bottom of project/target pane. A new window will appear. Select **iOS -> Apple Watch -> WatchKit App** and click **Next**. The next screen let's you configure options for your new target. Configure options and click **Finish**.

3. Now, you need a audio file. From Chapter 5 resources, drag the *gun_battle_sound.mp3* file into the **AudioExamples WatchKit Extension** group. Configure the options for new file similar to Figure 5-1.

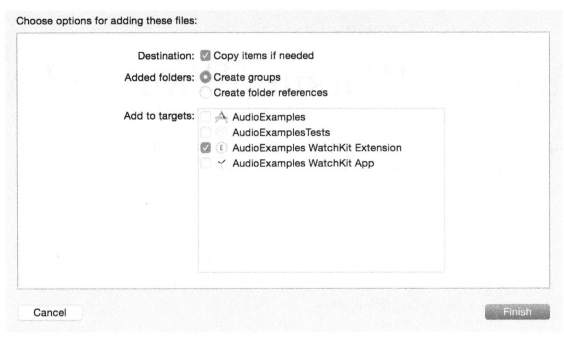

Choose options for adding these files:

Destination: ☑ Copy items if needed

Added folders: ⦿ Create groups
　　　　　　　○ Create folder references

Add to targets: ☐ ⒜ AudioExamples
　　　　　　　☐ ◌ AudioExamplesTests
　　　　　　　☑ ⒠ AudioExamples WatchKit Extension
　　　　　　　☐ ⅄ AudioExamples WatchKit App

Cancel　　　　　　　　　　　　　　　　　　　Finish

Figure 5-1

4. Select *InterfaceController.swift* file from *AudioExamples WatchKit Extension* group. Update the *InterfaceController.swift* file with the following code -

```swift
import WatchKit
import Foundation
import AVFoundation

class InterfaceController: WKInterfaceController {

    var audioPlayer = AVAudioPlayer()

    override func awakeWithContext(context: AnyObject?) {
        super.awakeWithContext(context)

        let filePath =
NSBundle.mainBundle().pathForResource("gun_battle_sound", ofType:
"mp3")
        audioPlayer = AVAudioPlayer(contentsOfURL:
NSURL(fileURLWithPath: filePath!), error: nil)
        audioPlayer.prepareToPlay()
        audioPlayer.play()
    }
}
```

5. Run the Watch app (make sure you select the WatchKit app scheme). We haven't added anything to storyboard yet, so you will see a black screen similar to Figure 5-2. But the audio file will be played as soon as the app starts.

Figure 5-2

How it works?

To play an audio file, we need to create an object of *AVAudioPlayer* class (a class written by Apple Engineers). The *AVAudioPlayer* class can be found within the *AVFoundation* framework.

We first import the *AVFoundation* framework as follows -

import **AVFoundation**

Once we write the above import statement, all the classes of *AVFoundation* framework, including the *AVAudioPlayer* class become available for us. We then create an object of *AVAudioPlayer* class and assign that to the variable named *audioPlayer* –

```
var audioPlayer = AVAudioPlayer()
```

We then add some code within the awakeWithContext(context:) method. The awakeWithContext(context:) method is called when the Interface Controller is loaded for the first time.

```
let filePath =
NSBundle.mainBundle().pathForResource("gun_battle_sound", ofType:
"mp3")
```

The above line gets the file path of *gun_battle_sound.mp3* file and assigns that to the constant named *filePath*.

```
audioPlayer = AVAudioPlayer(contentsOfURL: NSURL(fileURLWithPath:
filePath!), error: nil)
```

We then create an *AVAudioPlayer* instance with the contents of audio file and re-assign that to the variable *audioPlayer*.

```
audioPlayer.prepareToPlay()
audioPlayer.play()
```

The first line prepares the audio player for playback and the second line plays the sound.

Controlling Audio Playback

In this section, we will update the *AudioExamples* project so that it will not automatically play the audio. Instead, we will add buttons to control the audio playback. We will add buttons to start, pause and stop the audio playback.

1. Select *Interface.storyboard* file from *AudioExamples WatchKit App* group.

2. Drag three buttons from Object Library to the interface. Rename the button labels as "Start", "Pause" and "Stop" respectively (Figure 5-3).

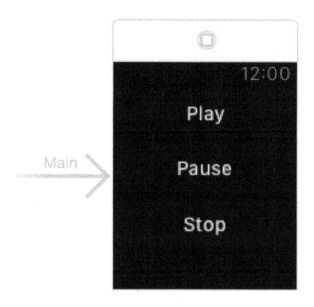

Figure 5-3

3. Click the Assistant Editor button and make sure the *Interface.storyboard* file is displayed in the main editor window and *InterfaceController.swift* file is displayed on the assistant editor window.

4. Add an Action for "Play" button by Ctrl-drag from button in storyboard to *InterfaceController.swift* file in the assistant editor. Set the **Name** field as **playButtonTapped** (Figure 5-4).

Figure 5-4

5. Add two more Actions, one for "Pause" button and another for "Stop" button. Set the **Name** field for those Actions as **pauseButtonTapped** and **stopButtonTapped** respectively.

6. Click the Standard Editor button and select *InterfaceController.swift* file. Remove the following line from awakeWithContext(context:) method –

```
audioPlayer.play()
```

We are removing this line from awakeWithContext(context:) method because we don't want to play the audio when the InterfaceController loads. Instead, we want to play audio when user taps the "Play" button. So, update playButtonTapped() action method with the following code –

```
@IBAction func playButtonTapped() {
    audioPlayer.play()
}
```

7. Update other two action methods with the following code –

```
@IBAction func pauseButtonTapped() {
    audioPlayer.pause()
}

@IBAction func stopButtonTapped() {
    audioPlayer.playAtTime(0)
    audioPlayer.stop()
}
```

8. Now save the changes and run the Watch app. You should see a screen like Figure 5-5.

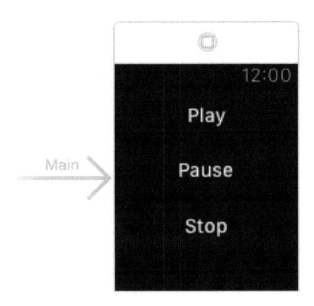

Figure 5-5

You will notice that audio doesn't play automatically. Instead, there are three buttons to control audio playback – Play, Pause and Stop. Tap these buttons and see how they work.

How it works?

We removed the following line from awakeWithContext(context:) method –

```
audioPlayer.play()
```

The play() method of *AVAudioPlayer* instance plays the audio. We want to play the audio once user taps "Play" button. That's why we added the above line to playButtonTapped() action method -

```
@IBAction func playButtonTapped() {
    audioPlayer.play()
}
```

To pause the audio playback, there is a pause() method of *AVAudioPlayer* instance –

```
@IBAction func pauseButtonTapped() {
    audioPlayer.pause()
}
```

Similarly, there is a method called stop(), which can be used to stop audio playback of *AVAudioPlayer* instance. But the stop() method doesn't reset the playback time, so you need to set it manually –

```
@IBAction func stopButtonTapped() {
    audioPlayer.playAtTime(0)
    audioPlayer.stop()
}
```

Controlling Playback Volume

In this section, we will make one last improvement to our *AudioExamples* project. We will add a slider to control the volume of audio playback.

1. Select *Interface.storyboard* file and drag a slider from Object Library to the interface (Figure 5-6).

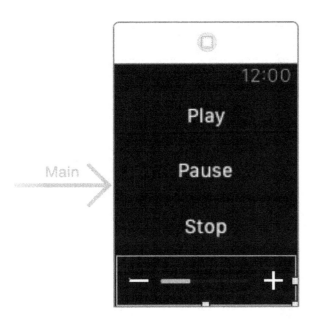

Figure 5-6

2. Click the Assistant Editor button and make sure the *Interface.storyboard* file is displayed in the main editor window and *InterfaceController.swift* file is displayed on assistant editor window.

3. Add an Action for slider by Ctrl-drag from slider in storyboard to *InterfaceController.swift* file in the assistant editor. Set the **Name** field as **volumeSliderTapped**.

4. Select *InterfaceController.swift* file and update volumeSliderTapped() action method with the following code –

```
@IBAction func volumeSliderTapped(value: Float) {
    audioPlayer.volume = value
}
```

5. Run the Watch app and you will see a volume slider at the bottom of the three buttons (Figure 5-7). Tap "Play" button to start the audio playback and use the slider to adjust volume.

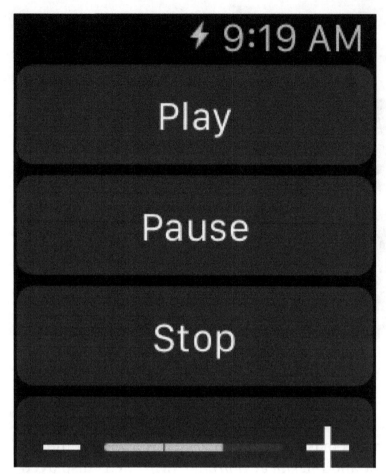

Figure 5-7

How it works?

The *volume* attribute of *AVAudioPlayer* instance let you set the volume of the audio playback. The value of *volume* can be any float value from 0.0 to 1.0.

When the user taps increment (+) or decrement (-) button of the slider, the volumeSliderTapped(value:) action method is called. The action method takes a parameter named *value*, which indicates the slider's current value (which can be a float value ranging from 0.0 to 1.0). So, we can set this value as *volume* of *audioPlayer* –

```
@IBAction func volumeSliderTapped(value: Float) {
    audioPlayer.volume = value
}
```

Demo App: Sound Effects

In this section, we will build an app which will allow us to play different sound effects.

1. Create an iOS app using the **Single View Application** template and name it "SoundEffects". Make sure you select **Swift** as **Language** and **iPhone** as **Device**.

2. Next, you need to add Watch App target to your iOS app. Select the project file in project navigator and click the + button at the bottom of project/target pane. A new window will appear. Select **iOS -> Apple Watch -> WatchKit App** and click **Next**. The next screen let's you configure options for your new target. Configure options and click **Finish**.

3. Now, you need to import audio files. From Chapter 5 resources, drag the directory named *"sounds"* into the **SoundEffects WatchKit Extension** group. Configure the options for new files similar to Figure 5-8.

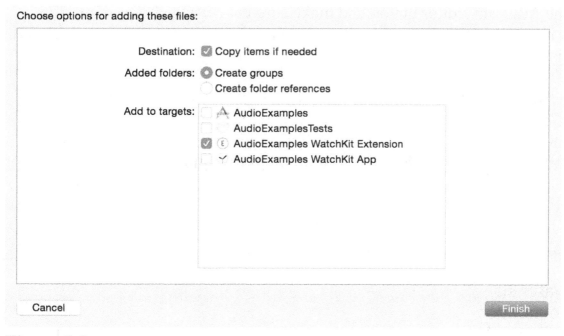

Figure 5-8

4. Select *Interface.storyboard* file from *SoundEffects WatchKit App* group. Drag three buttons from Object Library to the interface. Rename the buttons as "Rain", "Bird" and "Explosion" (Figure 5-9).

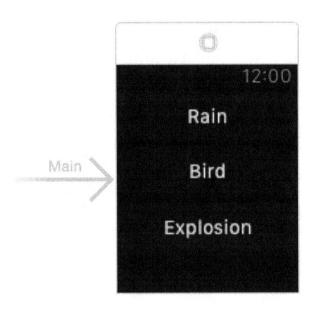

Figure 5-9

5. Click the Assistant Editor button and make sure the *Interface.storyboard* file is displayed in the main editor window and *InterfaceController.swift* file is displayed in the assistant editor window.

6. Add an Action for "Rain" button by Ctrl-drag from button in storyboard to *InterfaceController.swift* file in assistant editor. Set the **Name** field as **playRainSound**. Similarly, add two more actions for "Bird" and "Explosion" buttons and give the names **playBirdSound** and **playExplosionSound** respectively.

7. Switch to Standard Editor and select *InterfaceController.swift* file. Update *InterfaceController.swift* file with the following code –

```
import WatchKit
import Foundation
import AVFoundation

class InterfaceController: WKInterfaceController {
```

```swift
    var audioPlayer = AVAudioPlayer()

    func playSound(filename: String) {
        let filePath = NSBundle.mainBundle().pathForResource(filename,
ofType: "wav")
        audioPlayer = AVAudioPlayer(contentsOfURL:
NSURL(fileURLWithPath: filePath!), error: nil)
        audioPlayer.prepareToPlay()
        audioPlayer.play()
    }

    @IBAction func playRainSound() {
        playSound("rain")
    }

    @IBAction func playBirdSound() {
        playSound("bird")
    }

    @IBAction func playExplosionSound() {
        playSound("explosion")
    }

}
```

8. Run the Watch App and click any of the three buttons (Figure 5-10), you should hear the corresponding sound effect.

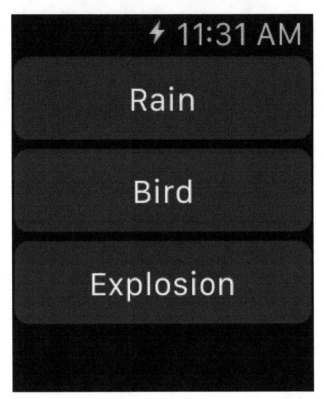

Figure 5-10

How it works?

We defined a function called playSound() as follows –

```
func playSound(filename: String) {
    let filePath = NSBundle.mainBundle().pathForResource(filename,
ofType: "wav")
    audioPlayer = AVAudioPlayer(contentsOfURL:
NSURL(fileURLWithPath: filePath!), error: nil)
    audioPlayer.prepareToPlay()
    audioPlayer.play()
}
```

A function is a self-contained chunk of code that performs a specific task. The function definition starts with the keyword "func", followed by the name of the function (in this case "playSound"), then a pair of parenthesis and finally the code inside curly braces. The pair of parenthesis after the function name can optionally contain one or more input values (called function parameters). When we need, we "call" the function by its name with value for function parameters (if there is any parameter).

The playSound() function takes one parameter – *filename*. The code within the playSound() function should look familiar to you, as it is very similar to the code you used in the previous example. The only difference is the use of the *filename* parameter.

```
let filePath = NSBundle.mainBundle().pathForResource(filename,
ofType: "wav")
```

When we call playSound() function, we provide a value for *filename*, e.g. playSound("rain"). In that case, the function parameter *filename* will be replaced by the value passed –

```
let filePath = NSBundle.mainBundle().pathForResource("rain", ofType:
"wav")
```

The rest of the code of playSound() prepares audioPlayer with the audio file of *filePath* and plays the audio.

Each of the three buttons correspond to an action method –

```
@IBAction func playRainSound() {
    playSound("rain")
}
```

Within the action method, we call the playSound() function with a filename and playSound() method does the work!

Summary

We have learnt how to play an audio file in our app. We later went on to add audio control and illustrated it in our Sound Effects demo app. In the next chapter, we discover how to work with tables in our Watch app.

Chapter 6: Tables

In this chapter, we will learn how to work with tables in our Watch apps. We will start by creating a WatchKit project and then add a table to our project. We will see how to add table contents like text labels and images.

Introducing Tables

We can use tables to display lists of data whose content changes dynamically. Using table to display data is a two step process – you first need to define layout for your data in the storyboard file and then write code to fill the table with actual data at runtime. Let's create a new project to demonstrate the process.

1. Create an iOS app using **Single View Application** template and name it "TablesExample". Make sure you select **Swift** as **Language** and **iPhone** as **Device**.

2. Now you need to add Watch App target to your iOS app. Select the project file in project navigator and click the + button at the bottom of project/target pane. A new window will appear, select **iOS -> Apple Watch -> WatchKit App** and click **Next**. The next screen let's you configure options for your new target. Configure options and click **Finish**.

3. Select *Interface.storyboard* file from *TableExamples WatchKit App* group.

4. Drag a Table object from Object library into your storyboard's interface controller scene (Figure 6-1).

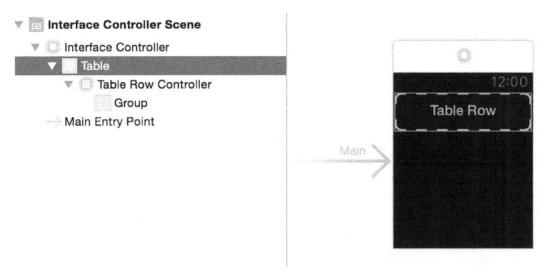

Figure 6-1

The table comes with a **Table Row Controller**, which is a template for displaying a single row of data in your table. You can use a row controller to display many rows. If you need, you can add additional row controllers for different kinds of rows.

Notice the row controller has a group inside it (Figure 6-1). You will add all of the row contents to this group.

5. Drag a Label from Object library into the table row group (Figure 6-2).

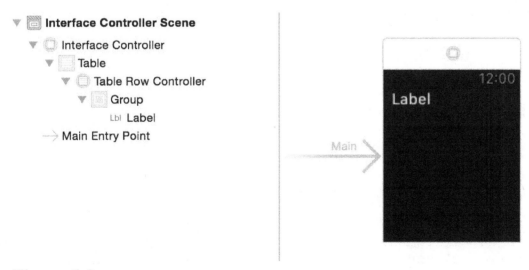

Figure 6-2

At this stage, you will expect to see a single row with a label when you run the app. But that's not the case, instead you will see a blank screen (Figure 6-3).

Figure 6-3

That's because table rows are filled with data at runtime and you need to write some code to make that happen!

Add Table Contents

Follow the steps below to add table contents –

1. Select *InterfaceController.swift* file and add an outlet for the table -

    @IBOutlet weak var **table:** WKInterfaceTable!

Now you need to connect the outlet in code with the table in storyboard. Select *Interface.storyboard*. Ctrl-drag from interface controller icon to the table (Figure 6-4), then select table from the Outlets popup to connect the outlet (Figure 6-5).

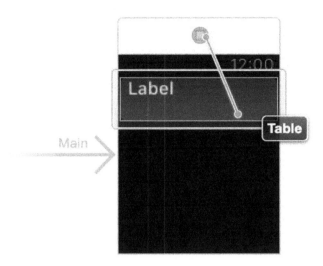

Figure 6-4

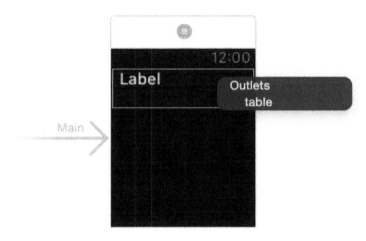

Figure 6-5

2. You need to add a custom class for the row controller. Right click on the *TableExamples WatchKit Extension* group and click New File. Select **iOS -> Source -> Swift File** template, name the new file *MyTableRow* and click **Create**. Select MyTableRow.swift file and add the following code –

```swift
import WatchKit

class MyTableRow: NSObject {
    @IBOutlet weak var label: WKInterfaceLabel!
}
```

Your table row is simply a subclass of *NSObject* class. First you need to import WatchKit framework and then declare an outlet for the label.

3. Next, select *Interface.storyboard* file and then select Table Row Controller in the Document Outline (Figure 6-6). Using the Identity inspector, change the class to *MyTableRow* (Figure 6-7). Then use the Attributes inspector to set the Identifier to *MyTableRow* as well (Figure 6-8).

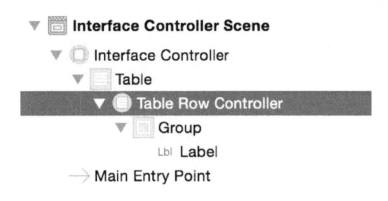

Figure 6-6

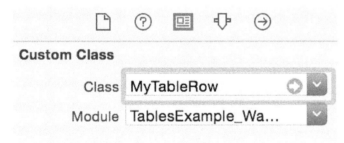

Figure 6-7

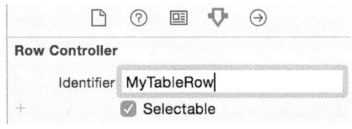

Figure 6-8

Here, you change the class of table row controller to the *MyTableRow* class that you created earlier. You also added an identifier for the table row. This identifier can be used to tell which type of row to create. Though you are using only one type of row for this app, you can add many different types of rows.

4. Now you need to connect the outlet of *MyTableRow.swift* file to the label inside the row. Ctrl-drag from *MyTableRow* in document outline to *Label* (Figure 6-9) and then select label outlet (Figure 6-10).

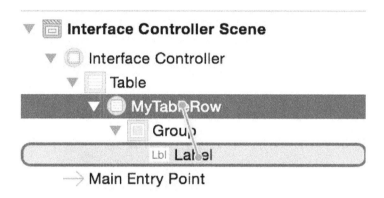

Figure 6-9

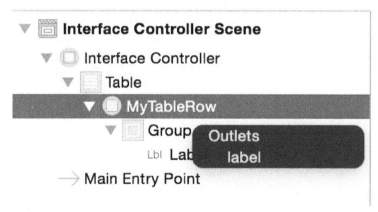

Figure 6-10

5. Update *InterfaceController.swift* file with the following code –

```
import WatchKit
import Foundation

class InterfaceController: WKInterfaceController {
```

```swift
@IBOutlet weak var table: WKInterfaceTable!

var rowTitles = ["Row 0", "Row 1", "Row 2", "Row 3", "Row 4"]

override func awakeWithContext(context: AnyObject?) {
    super.awakeWithContext(context)

    table.setNumberOfRows(rowTitles.count, withRowType:
"MyTableRow")

    for (index, title) in enumerate(rowTitles) {
        if let row = table.rowControllerAtIndex(index) as? MyTableRow
{
            row.label.setText(rowTitles[index])
        }
    }

}
}
```

6. Run Watch App. This time you will see five rows (Figure 6-11).

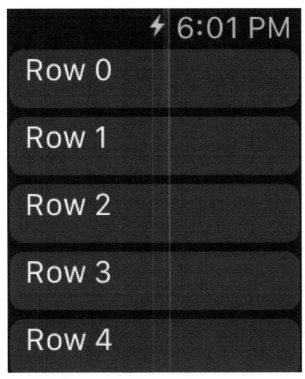

Figure 6-11

How it works?

We declared an array of string with five items –

    var **rowTitles** = ["Row 0", "Row 1", "Row 2", "Row 3", "Row 4"]

We want to set each item of this array as the label for each row. Next, we set the number of table rows and their type –

    table.setNumberOfRows(rowTitles.count, **withRowType:** "MyTableRow")

The type is the identifier we set on the table row in the storyboard. In our case, it is "MyTableRow". We get the number of rows by using the *count* property of *rowTitles* array.

We then enumerate through the items of *rowTitles* array. At this point, the table has already created five row objects and we use rowControllerAtIndex(_:) method to fetch the object for a particular row. Notice the *as?* operator, which ensures that we are only dealing with *MyTableRow* objects. Finally we set the text for row label with the items of *rowTitles* array.

```
for (index, title) in enumerate(rowTitles) {
    if let row = table.rowControllerAtIndex(index) as? MyTableRow {
        row.label.setText(rowTitles[index])
    }
}
```

Add Images to Table

In this section, we will see how to add images to table rows.

1. Drag an Image object from the Object library into the table row group and put it at the left side of the label (Figure 6-12). Using the Attributes inspector, set the width of image object to 50 points and height to "Relative to Container" (Figure 6-13).

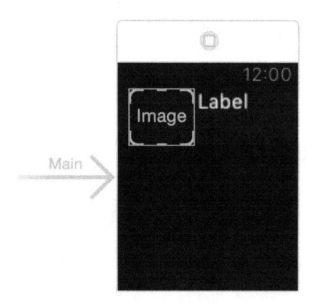

Figure 6-12

Size

Width	Fixed	
+	50	
Height	Relative to Container	
+	1	
+ Adjustment	0	

Figure 6-13

2. From Chapter 6 resources, drag *flower.png* image file into *TablesExample WatchKit App* group.

3. Select *MyTableRow.swift* file and declare an outlet for the image object –

@IBOutlet weak var **image: WKInterfaceImage!**

4. Now you need to connect the image outlet to the image object inside the row group. Select *Interface.storyboard* and ctrl-drag from *MyTableRow* in document outline to *Image* (Figure 6-14) and then select *image* outlet (Figure 6-15).

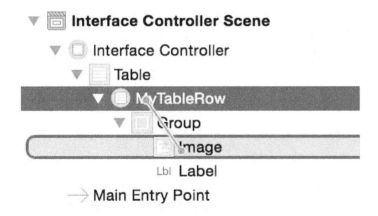

Figure 6-14

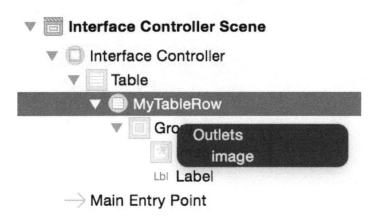

Figure 6-15

5. Finally, update awakeWithContext(_:) method of *InterfaceController.swift* file with the following highlighted line of code –

```
override func awakeWithContext(context: AnyObject?) {
    super.awakeWithContext(context)

    table.setNumberOfRows(rowTitles.count, withRowType:
"MyTableRow")

    for (index, title) in enumerate(rowTitles) {
        if let row = table.rowControllerAtIndex(index) as? MyTableRow {
            row.label.setText(rowTitles[index])
            row.image.setImageNamed("flower.png")
        }
    }
}
```

6. Run the Watch App. You will see a flower image shown at each row (Figure 6-16).

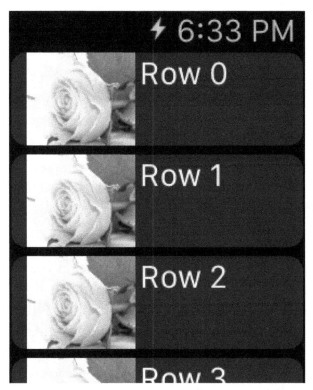

Figure 6-16

How it works?

We added an outlet for the Image object of row group -

@IBOutlet weak var **image:** WKInterfaceImage!

After that, we connected the outlet with the image object in storyboard. We next access the *image* outlet using the row controller –

row.image.setImageNamed("flower.png")

Here, we used setImageNamed() method of the image object to set an image for our table row. Though we used a single image for all rows, we could set different images for each row. The process of setting different images for each row is similar to setting different titles. Why don't you try it out? Here are some hints –

i.   Import 5 images to the *TablesExample WatchKit App* group

ii. Declare an array with image file names within the *InterfaceController.swift* file

iii. Set different images for different rows using the array of image names (e.g. rowImages[index])

Demo App: Friend List

In this section, we will build a demo table app. The app will display a list of friends. Each row of the table will show a picture and name of the person.

1. Create an iOS app using **Single View Application** template and name it "FriendList". Make sure you select **Swift** as **Language** and **iPhone** as **Device**.

2. Now you need to add Watch App target to your iOS app. Select the project file in project navigator and click the + button at the bottom of project/target pane. A new window will appear, select **iOS -> Apple Watch -> WatchKit App** and click **Next**. The next screen let's you configure options for your new target. Configure options and click **Finish**.

3. Select *Interface.storyboard* file from *FriendList WatchKit App* group.

4. Drag a Table object from Object library into your storyboard's interface controller scene (Figure 6-17).

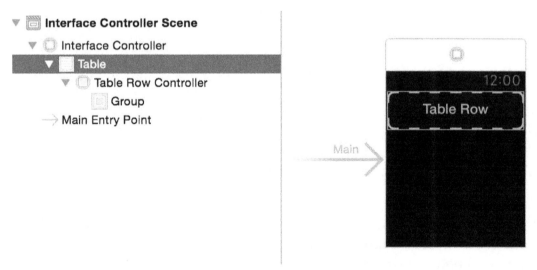

Figure 6-17

5. Select *InterfaceController.swift* file and add an outlet for the table -

@IBOutlet weak var **table: WKInterfaceTable!**

6. Select *Interface.storyboard*. Ctrl-drag from interface controller icon to the table (Figure 6-18), then select *table* from the Outlets popup to connect the outlet (Figure 6-19).

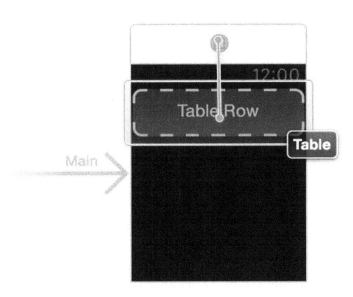

Figure 6-18

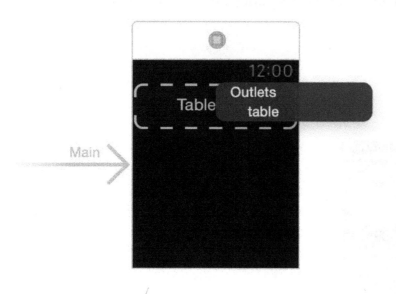

Figure 6-19

7. Drag an Image object and a Label from Object library into the table row group (Figure 6-20). Using the Attributes inspector, set the width of image object to 50 points and height to "Relative to Container". Next, import *images* directory from Chapter 6 resources to *FriendList WatchKit App* group.

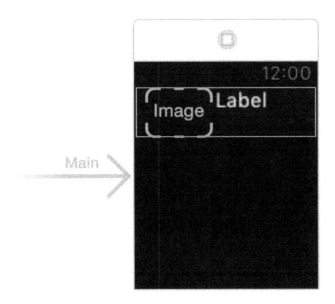

Figure 6-20

8. Add a custom class for the row controller. Right click on the *FriendList WatchKit Extension* group and click New File. Select **iOS -> Source -> Swift File** template. Name the new file *FriendRow* and click **Create**. Select *FriendRow.swift* file and add the following code –

```
import WatchKit

class FriendRow: NSObject {
    @IBOutlet weak var name: WKInterfaceLabel!
    @IBOutlet weak var photo: WKInterfaceImage!
}
```

9. Next, select *Interface.storyboard* file and select Table Row Controller in the Document Outline. Using the Identity inspector, change the class to *FriendRow* (Figure 6-21). Next use the Attributes inspector to set the Identifier to *FriendRow* (Figure 6-22).

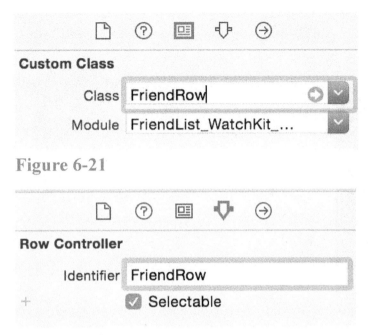

Figure 6-21

Figure 6-22

Here, you changed the class of table row controller to the *FriendRow* class that you created earlier. You also added an identifier for the table row. This identifier can be used to specify which type of row to create.

10. Now you need to connect the outlets of *FriendRow.swift* file to the label and image inside the row. Ctrl-drag from *FriendRow* in document outline to *Image* (Figure 6-23) and then select *photo* outlet (Figure 6-24).

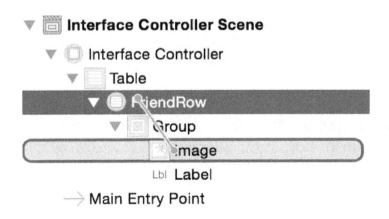

Figure 6-23

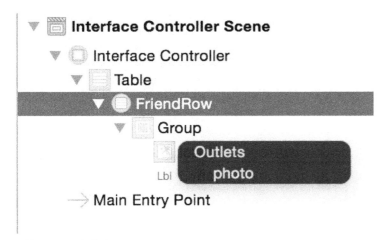

Figure 6-24

Similarly, connect the *name* outlet with *Label*.

11. Update *InterfaceController.swift* file with the following code –

```
import WatchKit
import Foundation

class InterfaceController: WKInterfaceController {

  @IBOutlet weak var table: WKInterfaceTable!

  var names = ["Alice", "John", "Kate", "Mike"]
  var photos = ["alice.png", "john.png", "kate.png", "mike.png"]

  override func awakeWithContext(context: AnyObject?) {
    super.awakeWithContext(context)

    table.setNumberOfRows(names.count, withRowType:
"FriendRow")

    for (index, name) in enumerate(names) {
      if let row = table.rowControllerAtIndex(index) as? FriendRow {
        row.name.setText(names[index])
        row.photo.setImageNamed(photos[index])
      }
    }
  }

}
```

}

12. Run the Watch App, you will see a screen similar to Figure 6-25.

Figure 6-25

How it works?

We added two outlets to *FriendRow.swift* class, which are connected to the image and label in table row group -

```
@IBOutlet weak var name: WKInterfaceLabel!
@IBOutlet weak var photo: WKInterfaceImage!
```

We declared two arrays, one containing the names and another one with image file names –

```
var names = ["Alice", "John", "Kate", "Mike"]
var photos = ["alice.png", "john.png", "kate.png", "mike.png"]
```

Next, we set the number of table rows and their type –

```
table.setNumberOfRows(names.count, withRowType: "FriendRow")
```

The type is the identifier we set in the table row in the storyboard. In our case it is "FriendRow". We get the number of rows by using the *count* property of *names* array.

We then enumerate through the items of *names* array. At this point the table has already created five row objects and we use rowControllerAtIndex(_:) method to fetch object for a particular row. We use the *as?* Operator to ensure that we are only dealing with *FriendRow* objects. Finally we set the names and corresponding images for each row -

```
row.name.setText(names[index])
row.photo.setImageNamed(photos[index])
```

Summary

In this chapter, we learnt how to add a table to our app. We went through the steps of adding text and images to each table row and finally illustrated the concepts with the Friend List demo app.

In the next chapter, we learn how to add multiple screens to our Watch app.

Chapter 7: Multi-screen App

So far, we have worked with single screen apps only. In this chapter, we will learn how to add another screen to our app. Once we add another screen to our app, we need to navigate between the screens. There are two ways to navigate between screens – navigating using storyboard segue and navigating programmatically. We will learn both techniques of navigation.

Adding a second screen

1. Create an iOS app using the **Single View Application** template and name it "MultiscreenAppDemo". Make sure you select **Swift** as **Language** and **iPhone** as **Device**.

2. Next, you need to add Watch App target to your iOS app. Select the project file in project navigator and click the + button at the bottom of project/target pane. A new window will appear, select **iOS -> Apple Watch -> WatchKit App** and click **Next**. The next screen let's you configure options for your new target. Configure the options and click **Finish**.

3. Before we add a second screen, let's add a button to the first screen. We want to use this button to navigate from the first screen to the second screen. Select *Interface.storyboard* file from *MultiscreenAppDemo WatchKit App* group. Drag a button from Object Library to the interface. Rename the button label as "Second Screen" (Figure 7-1).

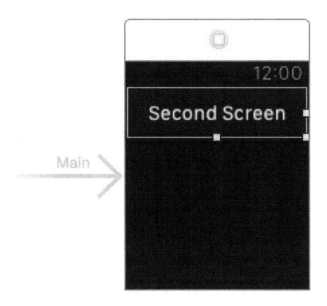

Figure 7-1

4. Now we are ready to add a new screen to our app. For each screen of our app, we need an Interface Controller. Drag an Interface Controller object from Object Library to the storyboard (Figure 7-2).

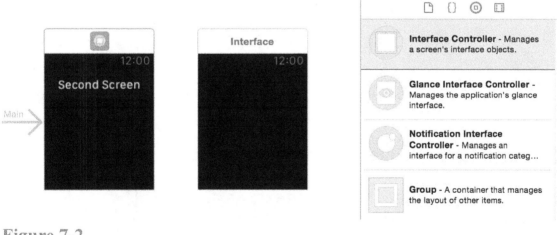

Figure 7-2

5. Next, add a custom class for our new Interface Controller. Add a new Swift file named *SecondInterfaceController.swift* to the *MultiscreenAppDemo WatchKit Extension* group. Make sure the **Class** name is *SecondInterfaceController*, **Subclass of** field has a value of *WKInterfaceController* and the **Language** is *Swift*

(Figure 7-3). Click **Next**. From the next screen, make sure both the **Group** and **Target** is *MultiscreenAppDemo WatchKit Extension.*

Figure 7-3

6. Update the content of *SecondInterfaceController.swift* file with the following code –

```swift
import WatchKit
import Foundation

class SecondInterfaceController: WKInterfaceController {

    override func awakeWithContext(context: AnyObject?) {
        super.awakeWithContext(context)
    }

    override func willActivate() {
        super.willActivate()
    }

    override func didDeactivate() {
```

```
    super.didDeactivate()
  }

}
```

7. Now we have a new Interface Controller in the storyboard and a custom class for that Interface Controller. But the Interface Controller in storyboard doesn't know anything about the custom class we created. So, select the new Interface Controller from storyboard and go to **Identity Inspector**. Set the **Class** field to *SecondInterfaceController* (Figure 7-4).

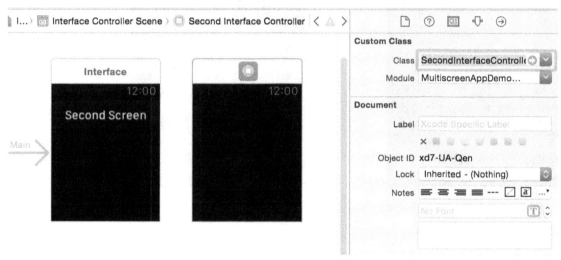

Figure 7-4

At this stage, we have a new Interface Controller in the storyboard and a custom class for that Interface Controller. But we don't yet have a way to navigate from the first screen to the second screen. Let's do that in the next section.

Segue from Storyboard

In this section, you will learn how to navigate from one screen to another by creating a segue. A segue is a connection which represents a transition from one screen to another.

1. Before we create a segue, let's first add some content to the second screen. Drag a label from Object Library to the second Interface Controller. Update the label's text to "Hello there!" (Figure 7-5).

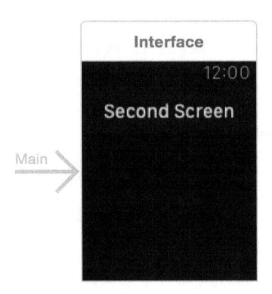 

Figure 7-5

2. Now select the button on the first Interface Controller and Ctrl-drag to the second Interface Controller (Figure 7-6).

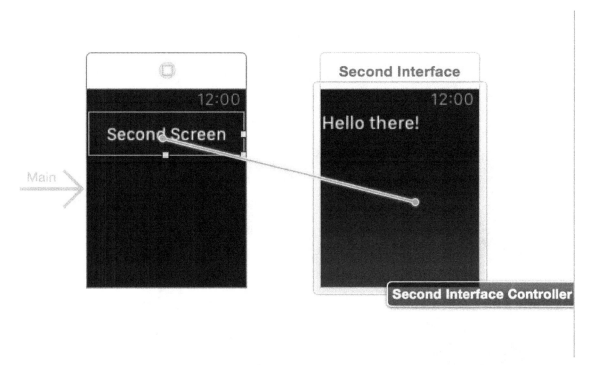

Figure 7-6

3. Release the mouse button and a small popup menu will appear (Figure 7-7).

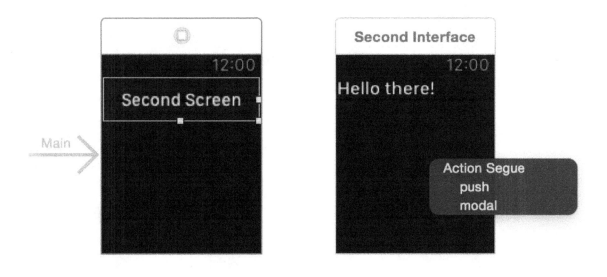

Figure 7-7

4. Choose 'push'. This will place a new arrow between the two Interface Controllers (Figure 7-8).

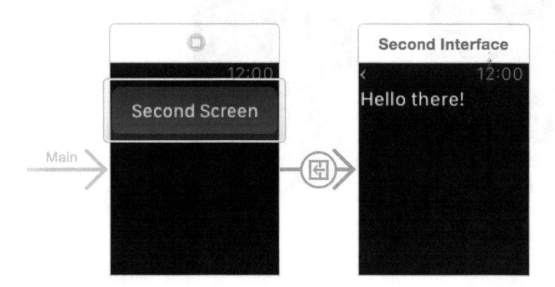

Figure 7-8

The arrow between the Interface Controllers is the segue, which represents the transition from the first screen to the second screen. This segue is triggered by the tap on the first screen button.

5. Now run the Watch app and tap on the button (Figure 7-9). As soon as you tap on the button, the app will transition from the first screen to the second screen (Figure 7-10).

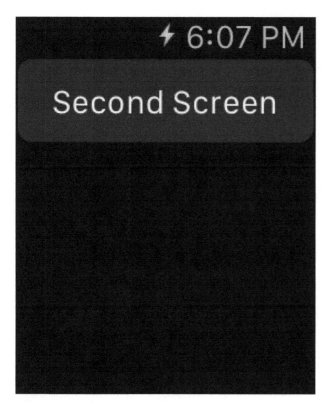

Figure 7-9

Figure 7-10

How it works?

We added a "push" segue from the first screen's button to the second screen. So, when the user taps on the first screen's button, the app will transit from the first screen to the second screen. We created a "push" segue that pushes the new screen from right to left. Once you navigate to a new screen using the "push" segue, you can return to the previous screen using the "back" arrow at the top left of the screen (Figure 7-10).

You can use another type of segue - the "modal" segue. Unlike the "push" segue, the "modal" segue appears modally which completely obscures the previous screen.

Segue from Code

In this section, you will learn how to navigate from one screen to another programmatically.

1. Add a new button to the first screen and change the button text to "Segue from Code" (Figure 7-11).

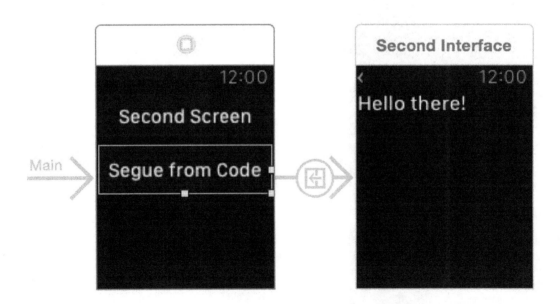

Figure 7-11

2. In order to navigate programmatically from the first screen to second screen, we need to give an identifier to the second Interface Controller. Select the second Interface Controller from the storyboard (make sure you select the yellow circle at the top of Interface Controller) and go to **Attributes Inspector**. You need to give an **Identifier** for the Interface Controller, enter "SecondController" (Figure 7-12).

Figure 7-12

3. Now select the first Interface Controller and click the Assistant Editor button. Make sure the *Interface.storyboard* file is displayed in the main editor window and *InterfaceController.swift* file is displayed in the assistant editor window.

4. Add an Action for "Segue from Code" button by Ctrl-drag from button in storyboard to *InterfaceController.swift* file in assistant editor. Set the **Name** field as **segueFromCode**.
5. Select *InterfaceController.swift* file and update *segueFromCode()* action method with the following code –

```
@IBAction func segueFromCode() {
    pushControllerWithName("SecondController", context: nil)
}
```

6. Save the changes and run the Watch app. Tap on "Segue from Code" button (Figure 7-13) and you will be taken to the second screen.

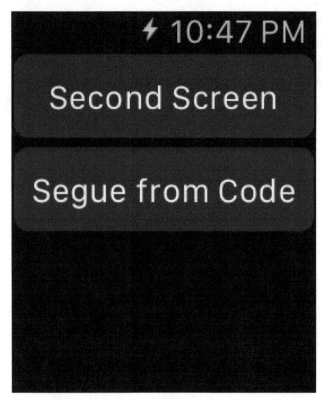

Figure 7-13

How it works?

The *pushControllerWithName(_:context:)* method performs a hierarchical navigation equivalent to using the push segue. You need to provide the destination Interface Controller's identifier in order to use this method. This identifier is set from the storyboard.

```
pushControllerWithName("SecondController", context: nil)
```

You can use the *context* argument to pass data to the destination Interface Controller. Since we are not passing any data, we used *nil* for this argument.

Demo App: Friend List v2

In this section, we will extend the *FriendList* app that we built in the previous chapter. We will add a second screen to the *FriendList* app. So, when the user taps on a table row, a detail page with that friend's information will be shown. Start by making a copy of *FriendList* project from the previous chapter and follow the steps below.

1. Drag an Interface Controller object from Object Library to the storyboard. Next, drag an image object and a label to the new interface controller scene (Figure 7-14)

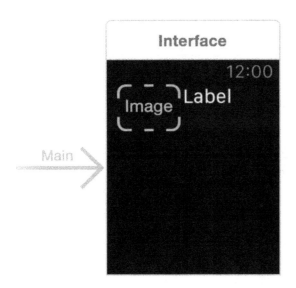 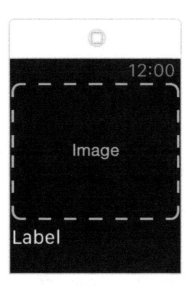

Figure 7-14

2. Next, let's add a custom class for our new Interface Controller. Add a new Swift file named *FriendDetailController.swift* to the *FriendList WatchKit Extension* group. Make sure the **Class** name is *FriendListDetailController*, **Subclass of** field has a value of *WKInterfaceController* and the **Language** is *Swift*. Click **Next**. From the next screen, make sure both the **Group** and **Target** is *FriendList WatchKit Extension*.

3. Update the content of *FriendDetailController.swift* file with the following code —

```
import WatchKit
import Foundation

class FriendDetailController: WKInterfaceController {

    @IBOutlet weak var nameLabel: WKInterfaceLabel!
```

```
@IBOutlet weak var friendImage: WKInterfaceImage!
override func awakeWithContext(context: AnyObject?) {
    super.awakeWithContext(context)

    if let name = (context as! NSDictionary)["name"] as? String {
        if let photo = (context as! NSDictionary)["photo"] as? String {
            nameLabel.setText(name)
            friendImage.setImageNamed(photo)
        }
    }
}
}
```

4. Select the new Interface Controller from storyboard and go to **Identity Inspector**. Set the **Class** field to *FriendDetailController* (Figure 7-15).

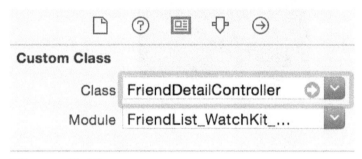

Figure 7-15

5. Select the second Interface Controller from storyboard (make sure you select the yellow circle at the top of Interface Controller) and go to **Attributes Inspector**. You need to give an **Identifier** for the Interface Controller, enter "FriendDetailController" (Figure 7-16).

Figure 7-16

6. Connect the outlet *friendImage* with the image object in storyboard and connect the outlet *nameLabel* with the label object.

7. Select *InterfaceController.swift* file and add the following method below the awakeWithContext(_:) method –

```
    override func table(table: WKInterfaceTable, didSelectRowAtIndex
rowIndex: Int) {
        pushControllerWithName("FriendDetailController", context: ["name":
        names[rowIndex], "photo": photos[rowIndex]])
    }
```

8. Now run the Watch App and tap on any row. You will see a detail screen similar to Figure 7-17.

Figure 7-17

How it works?

In our *InterfaceController.swift* file, we added the method table(_: didSelectRowAtIndex:). This method is called when a table row is selected. Within

127

this method, we called pushControllerWithName(_: context:) method to navigate to the second screen -

```
override func table(table: WKInterfaceTable, didSelectRowAtIndex
rowIndex: Int) {
    pushControllerWithName("FriendDetailController", context: ["name":
    names[rowIndex], "photo": photos[rowIndex]])
}
```

Notice that we passed a dictionary as value into the *context* parameter here. We use this dictionary to pass data to the second screen. We need to pass two values – name of the person and the image file name. The *rowIndex* parameter of table(_: didSelectRowAtIndex:) method gives us the selected table row index and use that *rowIndex* to get the name of person and image file name from the *names* and *photos* arrays.

The *context* dictionary which we passed from the first screen is received by awakeWithContext(_:) method of the second screen as a parameter –

```
override func awakeWithContext(context: AnyObject?) {
    super.awakeWithContext(context)

    if let name = (context as! NSDictionary)["name"] as? String {
        if let photo = (context as! NSDictionary)["photo"] as? String {
            nameLabel.setText(name)
            friendImage.setImageNamed(photo)
        }
    }
}
```

Here, we first get the values of *name* and *photo* from the *context* dictionary and then set those values to *nameLabel* and *friendImage* outlets.

Summary

In this chapter, we went through the steps of adding a second screen to our app. We learnt how to implement segues from both the Storyboard and from code. We applied these concepts in the extension of our Friend List demo app to show a friend's detail page when selected from a table row. In the next chapter, we will learn about glances.

Chapter 8: Glances

In this chapter, we will learn about glances. We will start by discussing what glances are and why they are useful. We will then create a Watch App project that includes a glance interface and see how we can run a glance interface using the simulator.

What are Glances?

From the *Apple Watch Human Interface Guidelines* -

"Glances are browsable collections of timely and contextually relevant moments from the wearer's favorite apps. Viewed together, glances are a way for people to get a quick look at content."

You can consider a glance as a supplemental way for the user to view important information from your app. A glance provides immediately relevant information in a timely manner. For example, the glance for a calendar app might show information about the user's next meeting.

User can access glances by swiping up on the watch face and then swiping left or right to see different glances.

WatchKit apps can only have one glance interface. Not all apps need a glance though. You should add a glance interface for your app only if it's relevant and offers additional value to user.

To learn more, you can read the *Glances* part of *Apple Watch Human Interface Guidelines* available at the following link –

https://developer.apple.com/watch/human-interface-guidelines/app-components/#glances

How to add a Glance?

In this section, we will create a new Apple Watch app that includes a glance interface. Follow the steps bellow –

1. Create an iOS app using the **Single View Application** template and name it "GlanceDemo". Make sure you select **Swift** as **Language** and **iPhone** as **Device**.

2. Now you need to add Watch App target to your iOS app. Select the project file in project navigator and click the + button at the bottom of project/target pane. A new window will appear. Select **iOS -> Apple Watch -> WatchKit App** and click **Next**. The next screen let's you configure options for your new target. Configure options similar to Figure 8-1 and click **Finish**. Make sure you check the **Include Glance Scene** check box.

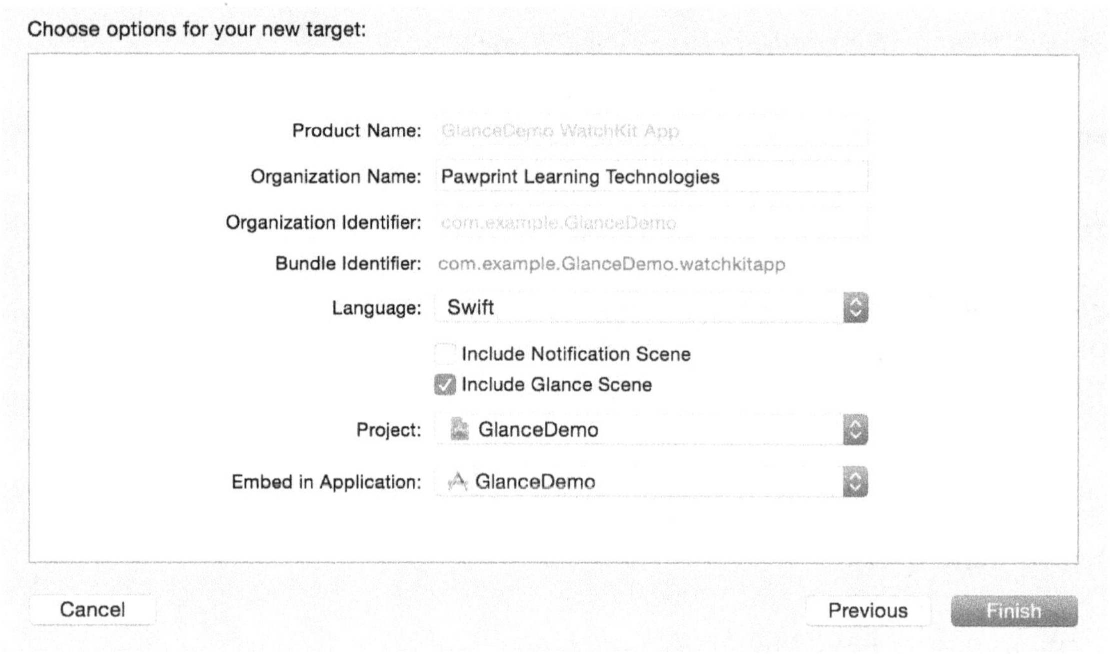

Choose options for your new target:

Product Name:	GlanceDemo WatchKit App
Organization Name:	Pawprint Learning Technologies
Organization Identifier:	com.example.GlanceDemo
Bundle Identifier:	com.example.GlanceDemo.watchkitapp
Language:	Swift
	☐ Include Notification Scene
	☑ Include Glance Scene
Project:	GlanceDemo
Embed in Application:	GlanceDemo

Cancel   Previous   Finish

Figure 8-1

Select the *Interface.storyboard* file. In addition to the Interface Controller Scene, you will see a **Glance Interface Controller** (Figure 8-2). You will also see a **GlanceController.swift** file in your *GlanceDemo WatchKit Extension* group (Figure 8-3). This *GlanceController.swift* file is mapped to the Glance Interface Controller.

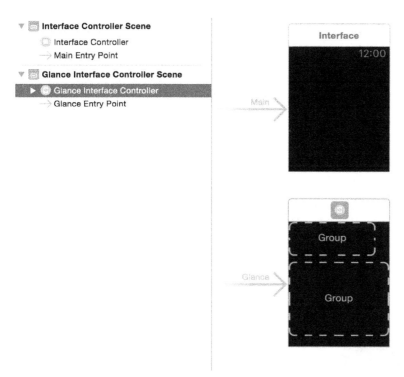

Figure 8-2

Figure 8-3

3. You can use the storyboard for the initial setup of your Glance interface. While setting up the Glance interface, you should remember the following two points from Apple's *Glance Interface Guidelines* –

- **Do not include interactive controls in your glance interface.** Interactive controls include buttons, switches, sliders, and menus.
- **Avoid tables and maps in your glance interface.** Although they are not prohibited, the limited space makes tables and maps less useful.

Let's add a label to our Glance interface. Select the *Interface.storyboard* file and drag a Label from the Object library into the storyboard's *Glance Interface Controller* (Figure 8-4).

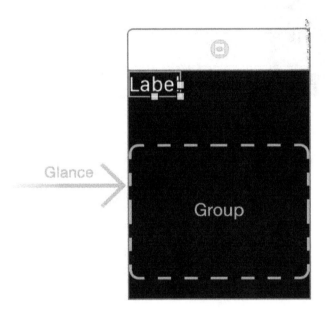

Figure 8-4

4. Next, we will add an Outlet for the label. Click the Assistant Editor button and make sure the *Interface.storyboard* is displayed in the main editor window and *GlanceController.swift* is displayed in the assistant editor window.

5. Add an **Outlet** for Label by Ctrl-drag from Label in storyboard to *GlanceController.swift* file in the assistant editor. Set the **Name** field as **label**.

6. Select GlanceController.swift file and update awakeWithContext(_:) method with the following highlighted line of code -

```
override func awakeWithContext(context: AnyObject?) {
    super.awakeWithContext(context)
```

```
    label.setText("My Glance Title")
}
```

As you can see, we have added a single line of code here. We use the setText()
method of *label* outlet to set a new text.

Now we are ready to run the Glance interface.

Running a Glance Interface

On the Apple Watch, users can swipe up to see the Glances. Unfortunately, the
Apple Watch Simulator doesn't support this type of interaction. But you can easily
test your Glance interfaces. To run a Glance interface, follow the steps below –

1. When you add an Watch App target with Glance Interface, Xcode automatically
creates a new scheme for you to test the Glance Interface. From the Xcode
toolbar's Scheme selector, select *Glance - GlanceDemo WatchKit App* scheme
(Figure 8-5).

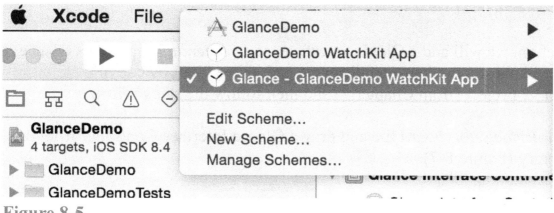

Figure 8-5

2. Now hit the Run button from the Xcode toolbar. You will see the Glance
interface appearing in the Watch simulator (Figure 8-6).

133

My Glance Title

Figure 8-6

Demo App: Friend List v3

In this section, we will add a Glance Interface to our *FriendList* app. This Glance Interface will show a random friend's name and image. Start by copying the *FriendList v2* project (from Chapter 7) and then follow the steps below.

1. Select *Interface.storyboard* file and drag a Glance Interface Controller from the Object library (Figure 8-7).

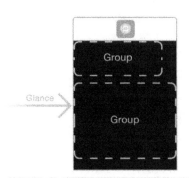

Figure 8-7

2. Drag a Label and an Image object from the Object library into the Glance Interface (Figure 8-8).

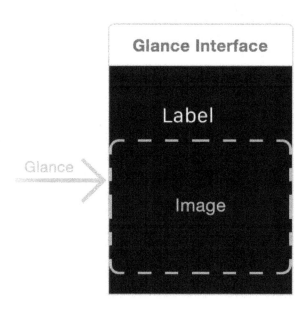

Figure 8-8

3. Next, add a custom class for the Glance Interface Controller. Add a new Swift file named *GlanceController.swift* to the *FriendList WatchKit Extension* group. Make sure both the **Group** and **Target** is *FriendList WatchKit Extension*.

4. Update GlanceController.swift file with the following code –

```
import WatchKit
import Foundation

class GlanceController: WKInterfaceController {

    var names = ["Alice", "John", "Kate", "Mike"]
    var photos = ["alice.png", "john.png", "kate.png", "mike.png"]

    @IBOutlet weak var nameLabel: WKInterfaceLabel!
    @IBOutlet weak var friendImage: WKInterfaceImage!

    override func awakeWithContext(context: AnyObject?) {
        super.awakeWithContext(context)
```

```
    var index = Int(arc4random_uniform(UInt32(names.count)))

    nameLabel.setText(names[index])
    friendImage.setImageNamed(photos[index])
  }
}
```

5. Select Glance Interface Controller from the storyboard and go to **Identity Inspector**. Set the **Class** field to *GlanceController* (Figure 8-9).

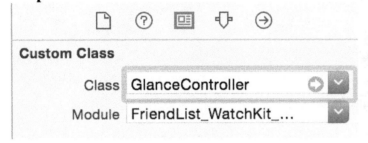

Figure 8-9

6. Connect the outlet *friendImage* with the image object in storyboard and connect the outlet *nameLabel* with the label object.

7. Now let's run the Glance Interface. Since we didn't include the Glance Scene while adding the Watch App target, Xcode didn't create a scheme for the Glance Scene. We will have to do that ourselves. From Xcode's scheme selector dropdown, select **Manage Schemes...** (Figure 8-10).

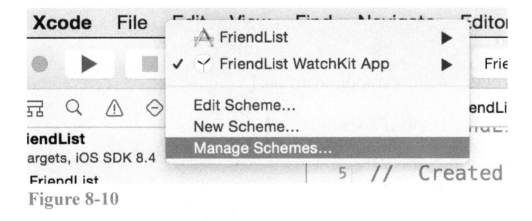

Figure 8-10

Next, select *FriendList WatchKit App* scheme and duplicate (Figure 8-11).

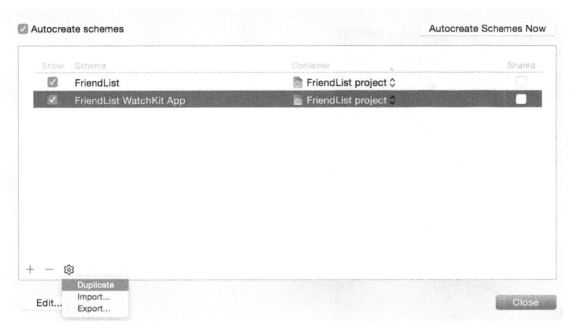

Figure 8-11

Configure the new scheme similar to Figure 8-12. Make sure you select *Glance* for the **Watch Interface** dropdown. Name the scheme as *Glance – FriendList WatchKit App*. Finally click **Close** button to save the newly created scheme.

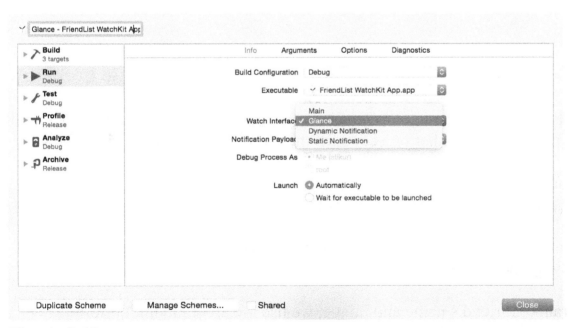

Figure 8-12

Finally, select the newly created *Glance – FriendList WatchKit App* scheme and run the app. You should see a screen similar to Figure 8-13.

Figure 8-13

How it works?

We added these two arrays in our *GlanceController.swift* file, one contains the name of friends and the other one contains the corresponding image file names –

```
var names = ["Alice", "John", "Kate", "Mike"]
var photos = ["alice.png", "john.png", "kate.png", "mike.png"]
```

We have also declared two outlets – one for displaying text label and another one for displaying the image.

To get a random friend's name and image, we use the arc4random_uniform() method to generate a random index between 0 and 3 -

```
var index = Int(arc4random_uniform(UInt32(names.count)))
```

Next, we use that index to get friend's name and image file name, and set values for *nameLabel* and *friendImage* outlets –

```
nameLabel.setText(names[index])
friendImage.setImageNamed(photos[index])
```

Summary

In this chapter, we learnt that glances are useful for a user to view immediate information from an app. We learnt how to implement them and applied that to our Friend List demo app. In the next chapter, we will learn about notifications.

Chapter 9: Notifications

In this chapter, we will learn about notifications on the Apple Watch. Apps can customize its notification interface and include custom graphics and content. We will learn how we can customize notification interface for our apps.

Notifications on Apple Watch

From the *Apple Watch Human Interface Guidelines* -

"Notifications on Apple Watch communicate high-value and immediate information through quick interactions. Notifications occur in two stages— short looks and long looks. The short look appears on wrist raise and contains brief but meaningful information about the notification. The lowering of the wearer's wrist causes the short look to disappear. If the wearer's wrist remains raised, Apple Watch displays a long look that provides more details about the notification."

If your iOS app supports notifications, Apple Watch automatically provides default short-look and long-look interfaces for the companion Watch App. The short-look interfaces are non-customizable. But you can customize your app's long-look interfaces and include custom graphics, additional content and custom color palettes. Users can either dismiss the notification or act on it by tapping an available action button (if there is any).

Working with Notifications

In this section, we will create a new Watch App project and see how to work with notifications. Follow the steps below –

1. Create an iOS app using **Single View Application** template and name it "NotificationsDemo". Make sure you select **Swift** as **Language** and **iPhone** as **Device**.

2. Now you need to add Watch App target to your iOS app. Select the project file in project navigator and click the + button at the bottom of project/target pane. A new

window will appear, select **iOS -> Apple Watch -> WatchKit App** and click **Next**. The next screen let's you configure options for your new target. Configure options similar to Figure 9-1 and click **Finish**. Make sure you check the **Include Notification Scene** check box.

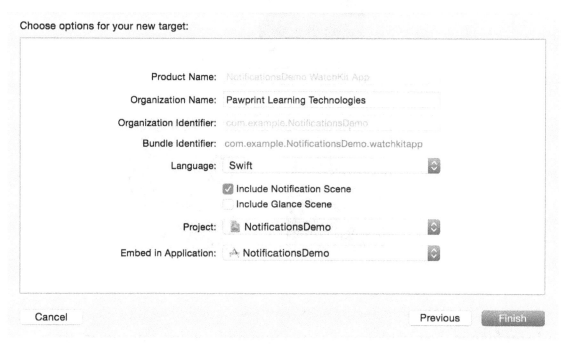

Choose options for your new target:

Product Name:	NotificationsDemo WatchKit App
Organization Name:	Pawprint Learning Technologies
Organization Identifier:	com.example.NotificationsDemo
Bundle Identifier:	com.example.NotificationsDemo.watchkitapp
Language:	Swift
	☑ Include Notification Scene
	☐ Include Glance Scene
Project:	NotificationsDemo
Embed in Application:	NotificationsDemo

Cancel   Previous   Finish

Figure 9-1

3. Select the *Interface.storyboard* file. In addition to the Interface Controller Scene, you will see a **Static** and a **Dynamic** notification interface (Figure 9-2).

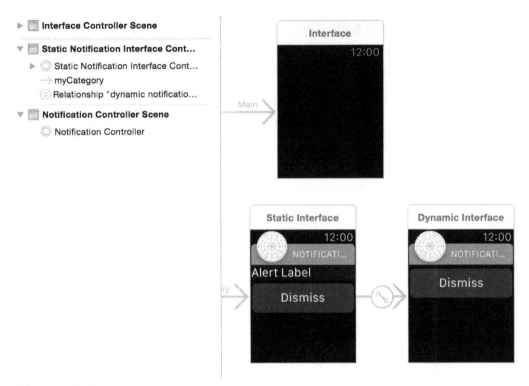

Figure 9-2

The **Static Interface** is the simpler among the two notification interfaces. It contains only the notification's alert message and static image and text. You cannot change the *Class* of your Static Interface, which means the elements of Static Interface can only be configured at design time (from the storyboard).

Unlike the Static Interface, the **Dynamic Interface** allows you to customize its contents at run time. If you expand the *NotificationsDemo WatchKit Extension* group, you will see a file named **NotificationController.swift** (Figure 9-3). This *NotificationController.swift* file is mapped to the Dynamic Interface. The Dynamic Interface displays a fully customized version of the notification's content and you can include custom contents and graphics if you want. While the Static Interface is required, Dynamic Interface isn't and you can delete it if you are not using it.

Figure 9-3

Testing Notification Interface

When you create a Watch App with a Notification Scene, Xcode automatically creates a new Scheme. Use the scheme selector dropdown from Xcode's toolbar and select **Notification – NotificationsDemo WatchKit App** scheme (Figure 9-4).

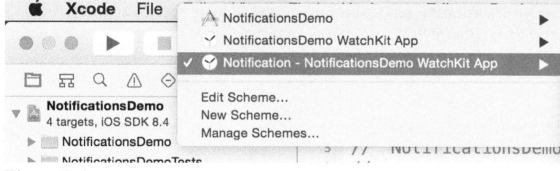

Figure 9-4

Now click the Run button and you will see the Notification Scene shown in the Watch Simulator (Figure 9-5).

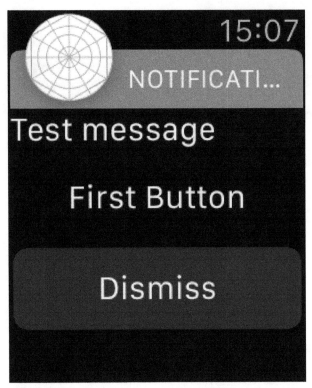

Figure 9-5

You might be wondering where all these data notifications come from. When you created the Watch App with Notification Scene, Xcode automatically creates a file named **PushNotificationPayload.json** for you to facilitate the testing of the Notification Scene (Figure 9-6).

Figure 9-6

144

Feel free to change some data of the above json file and re-run the app to see the updated contents!

Customize Notification Scene

You can't do a lot of customizations for Notification Scene except for a few items.

Watch App Icon

The image of Notification Scene is really the app icon of your Watch App. You can set an app icon for your Watch App by selecting the *Images.xcassets* file under the *NotificationsDemo WatchKit App* group and then selecting the *AppIcon* image set (Figure 9-7).

Figure 9-7

As you can see, you need icons of different sizes. You can learn more about icon sizes from the *Specifications* section of *Apple Watch Human Interface Guidelines* –

https://developer.apple.com/watch/human-interface-guidelines/specifications/

Display Name

To update the display name, select *Info.plist* file from *NotificationsDemo WatchKit App* group and change the value in the **Bundle display name** row (Figure 9-8).

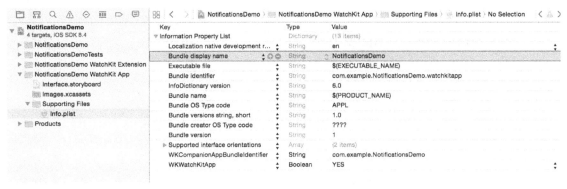

Figure 9-8

Color

To update color, select the Notification Interface and change the value of **Color** field in the attributes inspector (Figure 9-9).

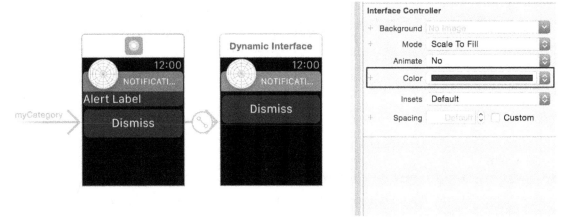

Figure 9-9

Background Image

You can provide a background image for your Notification Scene. To set a background image, select the Notification Scene and set an image for **Background** field from attributes inspector (Figure 9-10).

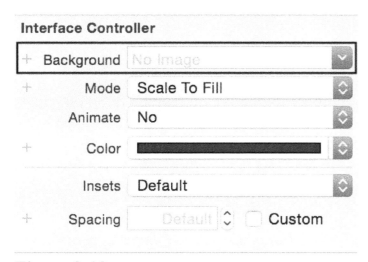

Figure 9-10

Where do Notifications come from?

You don't create notifications from your Watch app. Instead it's the job of your iOS app. Apple Watch displays notifications only if the containing iOS app supports them. If your iOS app supports notifications, Apple Watch displays those notifications automatically, you don't need to do anything from your Watch app (though you can customize the notification interface). When your app's notification (either local or remote notification) arrives on the user's iPhone, iOS decides whether to display that notification on the user's Phone or on the Watch.

If you want to know how to support local and remote notifications in your iOS app, you can check Apple's *Local and Remote Notification Programming Guide* –

https://developer.apple.com/library/prerelease/ios/documentation/ NetworkingInternet/Conceptual/RemoteNotificationsPG/Introduction.html#// apple_ref/doc/uid/TP40008194

Chapter 10: Working with Timers

In this chapter, we will learn how to use timers in our Watch Apps. WatchKit provides us with the *WKInterfaceTimer* class to create countdown or count-up timers. We will also learn about the *NSTimer* object and how to use it.

Timer

The Timer object (an instance of *WKInterfaceTimer* class) is a special type of label that displays a countdown or count-up timer. The Timer object lets you configure the amount of time and the appearance of the timer text. Once you start a timer, the displayed text is automatically updated on the user's Watch.

Let's create a new project to demonstrate how to use the timer in Watch App. Follow the steps below –

1. Create an iOS app using the **Single View Application** template and name it "TimersDemo". Make sure you select **Swift** as **Language** and **iPhone** as **Device**.

2. Now you need to add the Watch App target to your iOS app. Select the project file in project navigator and click the + button at the bottom of the project/target pane. A new window will appear. Select **iOS -> Apple Watch -> WatchKit App** and click **Next**. The next screen let's you configure options for your new target. Configure options and click **Finish**.

3. Drag a Timer from the object library into Interface Controller Scene. From the attributes inspector, change some attributes of timer. For the **Units** attribute, make sure that the only checked options are Second and Minute. Also change the value of **Preview Secs** to 20 (Figure 10-1).

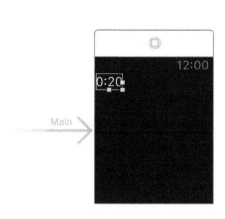

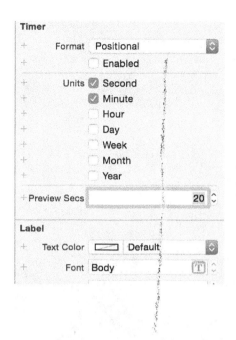

Figure 10-1

4. Click the Assistant Editor button and make sure the *Interface.storyboard* is displayed in the main editor window and *InterfaceController.swift* is displayed in the assistant editor window.

5. Add an **Outlet** for timer by Ctrl-drag from timer in storyboard to the *InterfaceController.swift* file in assistant editor. Set the **Name** field as **timer**.

6. Click the Standard editor button and select InterfaceController.swift file. Update awakeWithContext(_:) method with the following highlighted codes -

```
override func awakeWithContext(context: AnyObject?) {
    super.awakeWithContext(context)

    timer.setDate(NSDate(timeIntervalSinceNow: 20))
    timer.start()
}
```

7. Save changes and run the Watch App. You will see a countdown timer (Figure 10-2).

Figure 10-2

How it works?

We added an Outlet for the timer –

@IBOutlet weak var **timer**: WKInterfaceTimer!

We want our timer to countdown from 20 to 0. We used the setDate() method of timer to set the countdown duration –

timer.setDate(NSDate(timeIntervalSinceNow: 20))

The setDate() method takes an *NSDate* object. The following code returns an instance of *NSDate* class with date representing 20 seconds ahead relative to current date and time -

NSDate(timeIntervalSinceNow: 20)

After setting the time for countdown timer, we call the start() method of timer to start the countdown –

```
timer.start()
```

There is another method of timer called stop(), which can be used to stop the timer.

```
timer.stop()
```

NSTimer

When we work with timer, often we would like to get notified once the timer reaches zero. But the timer object (*WKInterfaceTimer*) provided by WatchKit doesn't offer that feature. In order to know when the timer reaches zero, we need to configure an *NSTimer* object with the same target date we use to set up the timer.

Select *InterfaceController.swift* file and make the following changes -

1. Add the following line below the *timer* outlet -

```
var intervalTimer: NSTimer!
```

2. Update awakeWithContext(_:) method with the highlighted lines of code –

```
override func awakeWithContext(context: AnyObject?) {
    super.awakeWithContext(context)

    timer.setDate(NSDate(timeIntervalSinceNow: 20))
    timer.start()

    intervalTimer = NSTimer.scheduledTimerWithTimeInterval(20,
target: self,
        selector: Selector("timeUp"), userInfo: nil, repeats: false)
}
```

3. Add a new method below the awakeWithContext(_:) –

```
func timeUp() {
    println("countdown completed!")
}
```

Finally, run the Watch App. You will see a countdown timer start and once the timer reaches zero, you will see a message in the Xcode console (Figure 10-3).

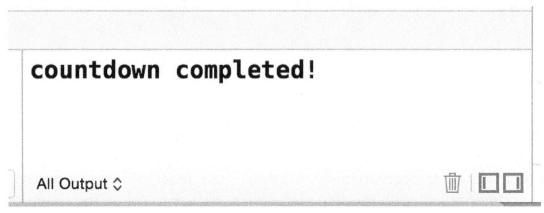

Figure 10-3

How it works?

We added a variable named *intervalTimer* which is an instance of *NSTimer* class -

```
var intervalTimer: NSTimer!
```

NSTimer class is used to create timers. Within our awakeWithContext(_:) method, we create a new timer by calling *scheduledTimerWithTimeInterval(_: target: selector: userInfo: repeats:)* method of *NSTimer* class -

```
intervalTimer = NSTimer.scheduledTimerWithTimeInterval(20, target:
self,
        selector: Selector("timeUp"), userInfo: nil, repeats: false)
```

The *scheduledTimerWithTimeInterval(_: target: selector: userInfo: repeats:)* method creates a new *NSTimer* instance and schedules it. This method takes a number of parameters. The first one is the number of seconds between firings of the timer. We specify 20 here because the other timer will also run for 20 seconds and we want to get notified after that time interval. The second parameter is the target, which is the object that get notified. The third parameter is method which is called when the timer fires. Once the timer fires, the *timeUp()* method will be called. For the final two parameters, since we don't have any user info, we passed *nil* as value and set repeats to *false* because we don't want to repeat the timer.

The timeUp() method will be called once the timer fires (after the countdown is finished) –

```
func timeUp() {
    println("countdown completed!")
}
```

This simple method prints a log message to the console. For a real world application, you will do whatever tasks within the above method when the countdown finishes.

Chapter 11: Submitting Your App to the App Store

This chapter will guide you to submitting your Watch app onto the App Store. To do so, you first need a paid Apple Developer Program.

Apple Developer Program

Join the paid Apple Developer Program at

https://developer.apple.com/programs/enroll/

Note that it costs $99 per year.

Figure 11-1

The Apple Developer Program allows you to submit apps for iPhone, iPad, Mac and Apple Watch onto the App Store. You will also get access to beta software, advanced app capabilities, extensive beta testing tools and app analytics. Do note that, if you want to deploy your own iOS app on your iPhone or iPad, you need the Apple Developer Program as well.

Setting Up your Developer Program Account with Xcode

Assuming you have already registered and paid for the Apple Developer Program (otherwise do so before you continue),

From the Xcode's menu bar, select **Xcode -> Preferences... -> Accounts** (Figure 11-2).

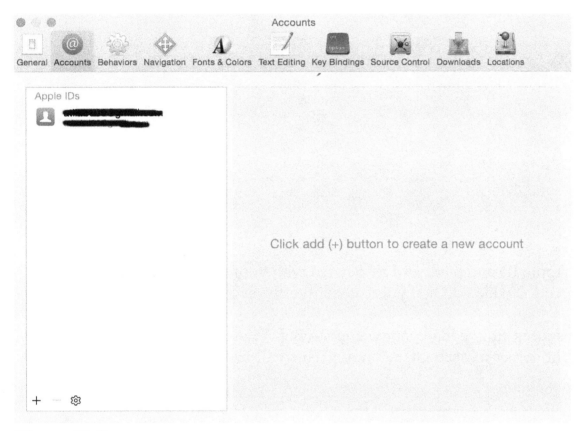

Figure 11-2

Now you will add your Apple ID associated with the Apple Developer Program. Click the + button at the bottom left corner of accounts tab and choose **Add Apple ID**. A new window will appear (Figure 11-3).

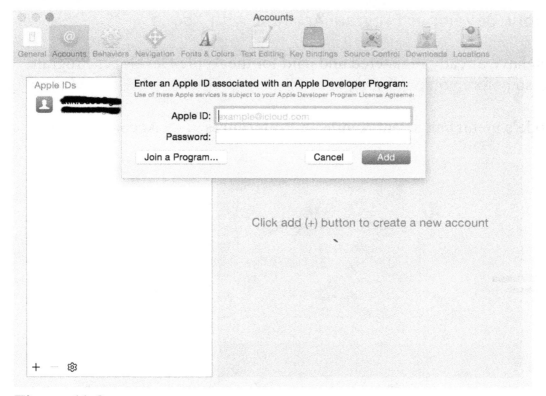

Figure 11-3

Enter the Apple ID and password associated with your Apple Developer Program and click **Add**. Xcode will add your account to the accounts window.

After you successfully added your account, click **View Details...** button (located at bottom-right corner of accounts window). This will bring up another panel (Figure 11-4).

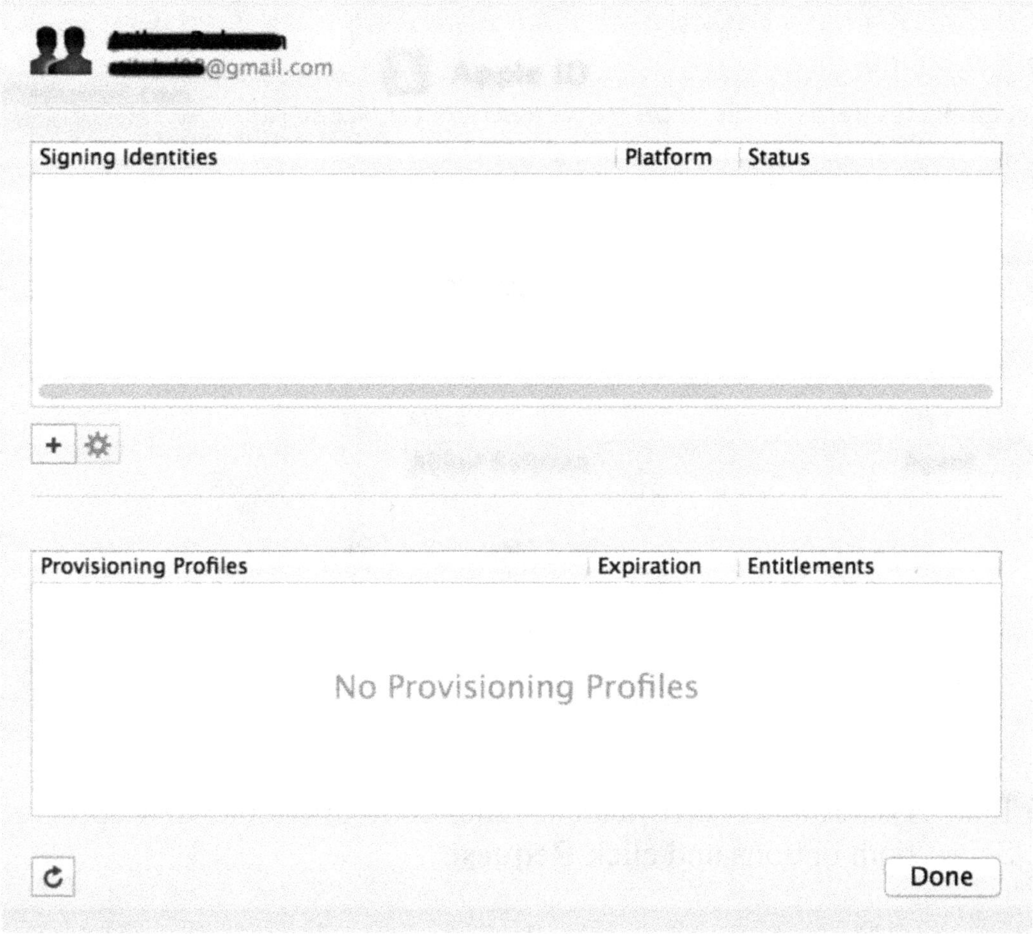

Figure 11-4

This panel lists your signing identities (certificates) and provisioning profiles. Currently this panel is empty. You need to click the little refresh button at the bottom-left corner and Xcode will attempt to contact the iOS Dev Center to fetch any certificates and provisioning profiles that you already have. Since you haven't created any of those yet, you should get a message similar to Figure 11-5.

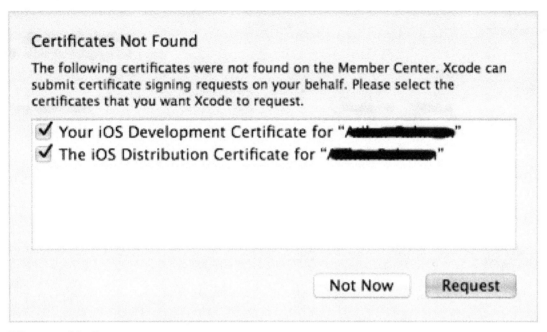

Figure 11-5

A development certificate is required if you want to run your iOS app onto your own iPhone or iPad. A distribution certificate is required to distribute your app via the App Store. Select both options and click **Request**.

Within a few moments, Xcode will automatically create two new certificates (a development certificate and a distribution certificate) for your developer account. Next, you need to create a distribution provisioning profile.

Create Provisioning Profile

A provisioning profile allows you to install apps onto your iOS devices. A provisioning profile includes signing certificates (which you already created in previous section), device identifiers and an App ID.

Visit the Apple Developer website, click "Member Center" and login with your Apple ID –

https://developer.apple.com/

Once you are logged in, click the "Certificates, Identifiers and Profiles' link (Figure 11-6).

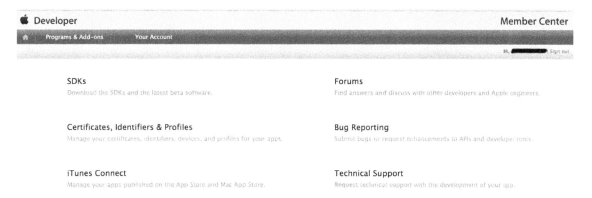

SDKs
Download the SDKs and the latest beta software.

Forums
Find answers and discuss with other developers and Apple engineers.

Certificates, Identifiers & Profiles
Manage your certificates, identifiers, devices, and profiles for your apps.

Bug Reporting
Submit bugs or request enhancements to APIs and developer tools.

iTunes Connect
Manage your apps published on the App Store and Mac App Store.

Technical Support
Request technical support with the development of your app.

Figure 11-6

In the next page under the iOS Apps section, select Provisioning Profiles (Figure 11-7).

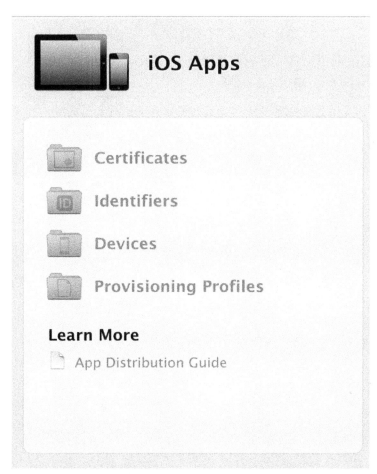

Figure 11-7

Click the + button to create a new provisioning profile (Figure 11-8).

Figure 11-8

You need to select the type of provisioning profile you are going to create. Under the distribution section, select **App Store** (Figure 11-9).

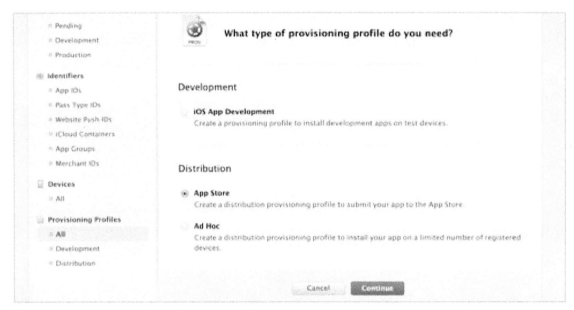

Figure 11-9

The next step will ask you to select an App ID. Since you don't have an App ID created already, you will need to create one. Click the **Create App ID** button (Figure 11-10).

Figure 11-10

App IDs are used to identify applications. Enter a description for the App ID (Figure 11-11).

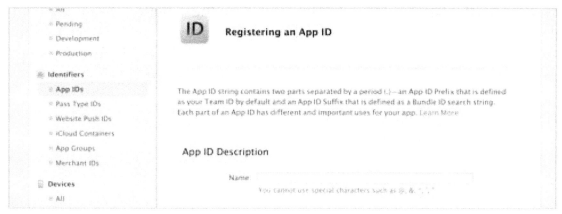

Figure 11-11

The **_App ID Prefix_** field will be automatically generated for you.

For **_App ID Suffix_** field, select Wildcard App ID and enter the value as

> *com.yourdomainname.**

(Replace com.yourdomainname with your own domain in reverse domain notation. This should match your organization identifier that you used while creating your app).

The asterisk (*) at the end represents that this single App ID can be used for all your apps.

Alternatively, you could have selected an *Explicit App ID*. In that case however, you have to create an individual App ID for each app you submit to App Store, like —

> *com.yourdomainname.appname1*
> *com.yourdomainname.appname2*
>   ...

If your app uses any special feature (like iCloud), you will have to create an *Explicit App ID*.

Click the **Continue** button and then complete the App ID creation process.

Now, let's return to the provisioning profile creation process. From the left panel, select **Provisioning Profiles -> Distribution** and click the + button. From the next screen, select the type of provisioning profile as **App Store** (under the distribution section) and click continue. (these are the same steps you followed before the App ID creation process). Now, the next screen lets you select an App ID (Figure 11-12).

Figure 11-12

Select the App ID you created earlier and click continue. In the next step, you will select the certificate. You should see the distribution certificate created from Xcode previously. Select the iOS distribution certificate and click continue (Figure 11-13).

Figure 11-13

The next step will let you generate the provisioning profile (Figure 11-14).

Figure 11-14

Give a profile name and click the **Generate** button. At this stage, your provisioning profile will be ready for download (Figure 11-15).

Figure 11-15

Download the provisioning profile and double click the downloaded file to install it.

From Xcode, go to **Preferences -> Accounts -> View Details** and you will see the provisioning profile shown (Figure 11-16).

Figure 11-16

You now have your distribution provisioning profile setup.

Preparing Your Build

Now we are ready to package it up to prepare for the App Store submission. From Xcode's Scheme selector, select the scheme for iOS app. From devices dropdown, select *iOS Device* (Figure 11-17).

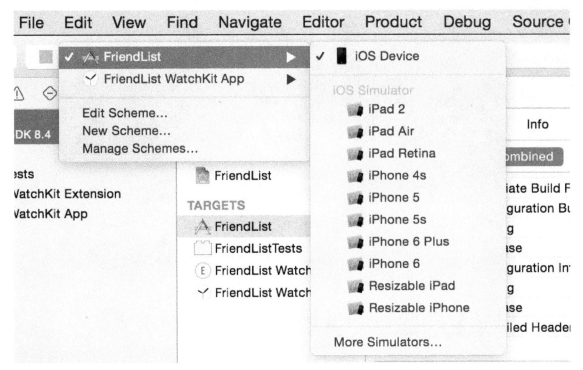

Figure 11-17

From the Xcode menu, click **Product -> Archive** (Figure 11-18).

Figure 11-18

Your app should appear in the Archives section of the Organizer (Figure 11-19).

Figure 11-19

Proceed to 'Validate' and 'Submit' your app to App Store.

Further details about submitting your app to App store are beyond the scope of this book. They are however readily available at developer.apple.com. You should also have a look at the following link, which contains extensive information about how to submit your Watch App to App Store –

https://developer.apple.com/app-store/watch/

Author's Note

Hello and thank you for reading our book. We would love to get your feedback, learning what you liked and didn't for us to improve. Please feel free to email us at support@i-ducate.com

If you didn't like the book, please email us and let us know how we could improve it. This book can only get better thanks to readers like you.

If you like the book, I would appreciate if you could leave us a review too.

Thank you and all the best to your learning journey in Apple Watch application development.